PAST LIVES, PRESENT DREAMS

How to Use Reincarnation for Personal Growth

DENISE LINN

BALLANTINE BOOKS • NEW YORK

Please note that *Past Lives, Present Dreams* reflects the personal experience of the author. If you intend to follow any of the exercises or suggestions in the book, it might be helpful to do so under the supervision of a therapist or other health care professional.

 Published in the United States by Ballantine Books, a division of Random House, Inc., New York, and simultaneously in Canada by Random House of Canada Limited, Toronto.

http://www.randomhouse.com

Originally published in somewhat different form in Great Britain in 1995 by Judy Piatkus (Publishers) Ltd. That edition was a new and expanded edition of *Past Lives, Present Dreams* published by Triple Five Publishing in Australia in 1988.

Library of Congress Catalog Card Number: tk

ISBN: 0-345-40002-X

Cover design by Min Choi
Text design by Ann Gold

Manufactured in the United States of America

First American Edition: March 1997

10 9 8 7 6 5 4 3 2 1

This book is dedicated to my husband, David,
and my daughter, Meadow . . .
fellow travelers through time and space

CONTENTS

Acknowledgments

Thank you, Leon Nacson, you are a true visionary.

Claire Brown, thank you for believing in me and my dreams.

Barb Kelly, it seems that we have known each other since the beginning of time. You are such a good friend.

Johnny Rozsa, you have made such a difference in so many lives.

Many thanks to Judy Piatkus, Gill Cormode, and Anne Lawrance at Piatkus Books for guiding this book to completion.

To Joanne Wyckoff, Andrea Schulz, and especially the wonderful anonymous copyeditor, my deepest thanks.

To my Cherokee uncle, Wade Scudder—though you are now with the Creator, I hear your whispers on the summer breeze and feel your kindness in the rising sun. I look forward to when we meet again "on the other side of the river."

INTRODUCTION: THE TIME IS NOW!

It is an exciting time to be alive. There has never been a more powerful time to step beyond our personal limitations, to step off the karmic treadmill into our full potential. It is only now, after aeons of evolutionary cycles, that each of us has the potential to come full circle into the blueprint of our own soul. The time is now. As we approach the end of the millennium, we can finally resolve old issues that began in past lives and use our dreams to step into our true domain.

The seeds for this book were planted many years ago by my teacher, Dancing Feather, of the Pueblo Indians. He was a humble man, yet he carried the great wisdom and power of his people within himself. This loving man helped me to connect more profoundly with my Cherokee heritage as he shared prophecies for our time and talked of the power of our dreams and the importance of releasing shadows from the past.

I remember being with him one warm summer evening as he sat cross-legged on the golden wild grasses of the sun-baked high mesa. This serene old medicine man was dressed in a faded cowboy shirt and well-worn jeans. A soft breeze rustled dried leaves, scattering them to either side of us. I strained to hear his gentle, low voice as he talked of the land and Mother Earth and Father Sky. His copper-colored face seemed to glow as it reflected the crimson sunset. His once jet-black hair was now a salt-and-pepper color. Deep age lines were etched across his face, yet when he spoke he had an animated, childlike humility that seemed to transcend time. Sometimes when he was talking he would stop and stare into the distance. His eyes, clouded with age, seemed to peer into some inner world for a moment. Then he would speak again.

He told me that Mother Earth was at the end of a long cycle, that we were at the time of completion and rebirth, and that huge changes were going to occur in the fabric of our lives. He said the renewal would be difficult for many people because right now people were lost. They had lost their roots and their ability to be in "right relationship" with all things. He said that people didn't know who they were. They had forgotten how to find themselves in each and every part of nature. This gentle being said we were the mountains, the great sky, the meadows, and the sea . . . we were all things great and small, but we had forgotten.

He talked of the importance of our dreams, for nocturnal journeys are an entrance point to the inner realms. In the years ahead, he said, our dreams would be a valuable source of inspiration and healing, playing an increasingly important role in our collective evolution. He also explained that it would become essential to release the shadows of pain, suffering, and wounds from the past, as these were keeping us from experiencing fully the beauty around us. He said it was crucial that we learn to listen to our inner wisdom and to the spirit ancestors and guides around us and that we must "reach for the stars" and remember who we are. He was excited about the great potential for us all in the time ahead.

Over the years since Dancing Feather's death, I have seen the wisdom of his words. Our planet is indeed changing very quickly, just as he prophesied. As we face the end of the millennium, huge changes in technology and our natural resources are taking place. This rapid change is deeply affecting the way in which we relate to one another and to our environment. We have forgotten the primordial knowledge that all creatures and all things on earth are connected. We have forgotten that we are all connected to a living, pulsating universe—a universe that is no less alive than the majestic whales in the sea or the wild flowers opening to the sun on the hillsides. We have forgotten that we live in a universe that sings with life, that pulses with intensity of Spirit.

The universe is just as much alive as our human bodies. When we suffer injury to a part of ourselves, the entire body responds by sending healing energy to the site of the distress. We are not aware of the myriad biochemical processes that occur in the body's immune system. However, when we are injured, the body responds automatically: it is a natural response. This is the nature of life . . . this is the nature of the universe.

The human body is a microcosm of the macrocosm of the universe; our planet can be likened to one cell in the body of the living universe. Right now, our planet is injured. The universe is sending healing energy to our planet in the same way as the human immune system becomes activated when there is injury to the body. As wave after wave of healing energy infiltrates our planet, a massive purification begins to take place, causing a cosmic stirring up of old structures and institutions and limiting beliefs.

Global purification can be likened to the cleansing of a deep pond of stagnant water. The top few inches appear clear, but below the surface the pond is choked with silt and unhealthy growth. Suddenly there is a surging infusion of fresh, clear water from springs below. All the fetid water is churned up. The short-term effects seem chaotic, and all is in turmoil. The pond looks worse—it is muddy and foul with decaying matter. However, the purification is essential for the health of the pond, which soon becomes crystal clear and sweet. Today, our planet is not unlike that stagnant pond. The new frequencies that are being projected to the earth can be likened to the fresh springs that cause upheaval as they create an incredible cleansing and clearing.

As we face the exciting and challenging times ahead, we have enormous potential to release the heavy burdens we have carried through lifetime after lifetime. The cosmic stirring up of old structures and hierarchies means that old blockages are currently surfacing. As new energies flood the planet, many people are experiencing an intense resurgence of old issues, which results in temporary feelings of disorientation and upheaval. Many are dealing with and resolving their grief and rage over old issues that had long been suppressed or denied.

Denial of pain and suffering in this life, *as well as in previous lives,* is coming to light now. Many people are struggling to overcome their barriers to wholeness. All the suffering, fear, and pain of separation that have accrued within us over countless lifetimes, and that exist inside us as suppressed memories, are now crying for release. Now, we have the opportunity to let go of these old limitations from the past.

Deep within each of us is a vast, interconnected universe where the past and present and future swirl in a great orchestration of light and sound. As we approach the end of the millennium, the veil between our personal inner universes and the outer universe around us is thinning. We have the opportunity to step through our dreamtime portals into the mysterious realms of self and see the inner truths that have been hidden from us for so long.

The challenge, in the years to come, is to be willing to confront your shadow, to be willing to step through the veil of the night with courage and an open heart, and to face who you have been in past lives, so that you can live more richly in the present. There are many shadows that present themselves in our lives—fear, pain, sadness, self-limiting beliefs, disease, and death. These shadows usually have their source in past lives. The journey beyond the shadows takes only the willingness to risk. And only those who risk will truly live. Your journeys into past lives can be turning points in life and can bring about the deepest levels of transformation.

As the nocturnal door between the past, present, and future is opening, you can use your dreams to reveal and to heal the shadows of your past lives. In doing so, you prepare in the very depth of your being to face the coming challenges with grace and ease. You can also use your past life explorations and your dreamtime journeys to move into the universal essence from which all life, all thought, and all existence flow.

This process is the ancient and sacred journey of the soul in search of itself. Once you have chosen this path, you may not return. However, it is a path that, once taken, will enhance your ability to experience powerful depths of love—love for self, for others, and for your planet. It is a path that can help you to make a difference in the world.

About This Book

As the changes to our planet increase, your past lives and your dreams can be an increasing source of transformation and inspiration. But how can you best take advantage of the energies now available for growth and personal expansion? How can you remember who you were in a past life or release negative programming from past lives? How can you remember your dreams and know what they are trying to tell you? And why is this such an important time in history? *Past Lives, Present Dreams* gives you simple, viable answers and solutions.

You *can* remember who you were in a past life. Anyone can. This book offers simple techniques to help you recall events from your past lives. It also explains reincarnation and karma and why they are so important at this time. You will learn how to use past-life "clues" to discover who you were in past incarnations. This book shows how to use past-life therapy to release persistent conditions such as current fears and phobias, relationship difficulties, blockages to abundance and creativity, and physical ailments. In the following pages you will find specific techniques to resolve and release current difficulties that originated in past lives. In addition, you will read about the different kinds of spirit guides and learn exercises that enable you to get in touch with them.

As our planet's vibratory rate continues to accelerate, it is vital that you listen to the messages in your dreams, for each one carries messages from your soul that can help you to stay in balance in the coming years. Your dreams can assist the inner and outer healing that is taking place now. This book teaches you how to program, remember, and interpret your dreams. In addition, you will learn how to use your dreams for past-life explorations.

Examples of past-life regressions are given throughout this

book. Some of them are from my clients, while others are from letters and conversations with people who attended my past-life seminars. In some cases I have quoted exactly from letters. Where I have paraphrased or shortened the description for easier reading, I have tried to be as close to the spirit of the person's experience as possible.

As we approach the new millennium, huge and exciting changes will occur on many levels within our multidimensional universe. These changes have been foretold by native cultures around the world, and as they take place it will be exceedingly valuable for you to find an oasis of inner peace within yourself. The aim of this book is to give you information and techniques to prepare you for the future. We are all the spiritual heirs of the planet, and the extent to which you can release blockages and limitations from the past and listen to your dreams and inner guidance is the extent to which you can step into the future with love. Only then can there be order and joy in the cosmos.

1.
MY JOURNEY INTO PAST LIVES AND DREAMS

My journey began very dramatically when I was seventeen, in the summer of 1967. I was riding my motorbike on a country road in our small farming community in the Midwest. It was a hazy, peaceful day. My hair blowing in the wind, I flew past great fields of golden maize. Then, abruptly, my serenity was shattered.

A car rear-ended me, throwing me violently to the ground. As I struggled to my feet, I saw a man aiming a gun at me. The dark barrel of the gun seemed enormous.

Just before I was shot, a thought raced across my brain: He's aiming too low. A split second later I was left lying on the side of the road. A farmer found me and called an ambulance.

Harsh, bright hospital lights. Sharp pain. Shrill voices. Then slowly the lights began to dim and the pain subsided. I felt myself slip into a comfortable, soft blackness where I rested in a bubblelike cocoon. It was at this point, I was told later, that the doctors thought I had died.

Suddenly, the bubble seemed to burst and I was bathed in a glorious, golden light. In fact, I wasn't just bathed in light—I *was* the light, all-pervading and luminous. I then became aware of unbelievably sweet and pure music—ebbing and flowing sound waves of liquid light that pervaded my spirit until I actually became the music. It seemed in that moment that I was made of nothing but fluid light and sound. And the light and sound were not separate from each other, but merged together as one.

I had no sense of time. Everything existed in the infinite present. The past was inconceivable. It was as difficult to imagine linear time there as it is for me to experience nonlinear time here. Everything just *was*.

I was also overwhelmed with a deep sense of familiarity. I knew I had been there before. It was the most real thing that I had ever experienced. The glorious realm I had entered was the only reality.

Infused in this light and sound and infinite "nowness" was a most perfect love. I felt, at the very heart of my being, a kind of love that was as natural as breathing. It was a love beyond form, like the universe itself, penetrating every aspect of the self.

And I wasn't alone. You were there, too—in fact, there wasn't anyone or anything that wasn't there. We were all there. Without bounds, without separation. I was everyone, and everyone was me. We were all one. Feeling no longer bound to my body, I experienced boundlessness and a sense of unity with all of life. I had come home.

I saw in front of me a great river emitting a soft golden light. As I looked to the far shore, I knew that when I reached it I would never return to my seventeen-year-old body. I had never been happier.

When I was halfway across the river, shimmering fluid light

parted on either side of me. But as I reveled in my homecoming, a deep and ominous voice boomed, "You may not stay here. There is something you still need to do." But even as my mind screamed, *Nooo!* it seemed that I had been lassoed and was being dragged back to my physical body.

I woke up in my hospital bed. Day after day I fought for my life, struggling not only with physical pain but with tremendous grief over returning to my body. Every evening, however, I experienced a miracle. After the lights had been turned down and I was alone, I would close my eyes and I would feel a hand slip gently into mine. A wonderful feeling of comfort and safety would flood my being. When this happened, I would sometimes open my eyes and look at my hand. Although I couldn't see the hand that held mine, I actually felt the contours of fingers and palm and a radiating warmth. Sometimes the hand would release mine and a different hand would fold lovingly into it. I particularly remember a very small, childlike hand comforting me one night. I knew I was safe. I knew I wasn't alone. I believe those hands belonged to angels.

The doctors thought I would not survive. The bullet had bounced off my spine, lodging in a lung after tearing away my spleen, an adrenal gland, and damaging my stomach and intestines. Eventually one of my kidneys was removed and a plastic tube was inserted to replace my aorta. But during those few minutes when they thought I was dead, that shift in my consciousness altered the course of my life forever, allowing for my survival and rapid recovery. I feel that in those mysterious and magical few moments, part of my previous identity was removed from my soul. This helped me to heal, because I experienced that I was more than my body. I knew I was light and spirit and music and energy and love. The awareness made it much easier to heal my body. I realized my body wasn't "me." It was something that part of me inhabited, but I was much more than my body. I had many more resources to heal myself than just those available to my physical body.

A Changed Life

After my "near-death experience," my sense of self shifted, completely altering my life. After I was shot, I no longer believed that when my body died, I died. I no longer thought that my existence began at conception and ended at death. I was no longer separate from everything and everyone else on the planet. Time wasn't linear anymore, nor was the universe governed by fixed rules of physics. The shift in my consciousness changed forever my beliefs about the nature of reality.

Although the world around me looked physically the same, my experience of it was completely different. Life became very precious. Every moment was full of color and form and sound and vibrant energy. Each blade of grass shimmered in its own light, singing its own song; a field of wild grasses was like a great orchestra of light and music. Trees had a deep, sonorous hum, and leaves unfurled to warm winds that felt like the breath of God. Even the earth beneath my feet pulsed with the gentle cadence of life. I had great difficulty understanding that most people couldn't feel and see the overwhelming beauty around them. I couldn't comprehend cruelty or violence. I knew that we were part of one huge, vibrant, living universe, and that we couldn't hurt others without hurting ourselves.

As a result of my near-death experience, I now believe that we are infinite and eternal, and that we are all intimately connected—cosmically linked, so to speak. I can't truly get home until you do, and vice versa. I also believe that time is malleable and changeable, so that we can change the past as well as the future. I believe in God and angels and guides. I believe that we have all experienced past lives, and that our dreams can be a powerful source of inspiration and healing. I now know that we all have an innate ability to create and manifest the universe around us. In fact, that we are subconsciously creating it right now through our thoughts, feelings, and the core beliefs that we have carried forward from other lifetimes.

Thousands of people have had experiences similar to mine, and certain elements are common to most of them. The initial stages of the near-death experience usually involve a sense of deep peace and a feeling of being unattached to the body or of floating above it. Many people feel that they are sucked into a tunnel with a light at the far end of it, where they are greeted by beings of light or by people whom they know but who had died. In almost all cases, these people feel very loved and cared for. Often, individuals have the opportunity to review their lives from an observer's point of view. Almost always they feel that they hadn't completed what they needed to do on earth, yet there is a tremendous reluctance to return to the body.

Research has shown that those who have had such experiences share some traits and, in almost all cases, have been changed by the event. They tend to fear death less than do most people. On the whole, they experience a greater sense of inner peace and a greater zest for living. In addition, they are often drawn toward the caring professions.

I am not special in having had a near-death experience. I think that in my case, I was so far off my spiritual path that it took a cosmic kick to get me on my path. I believe that the universe is always whispering to us. If we don't listen to the whispers, we'll hear the screams. My experience was like a huge shout from Spirit: "Denise, remember who you are!"

That shout continues to echo in my life. I came back to life with the knowledge that this is the most important time in the evolution of our planet. I now understand that the growth, individually and collectively, of our consciousness is essential for the future of our planet. I developed a deep desire to understand life in the light of the past lives that we have lived, having learned that knowledge of past lives can open the door to deep personal healing. I know that we are never alone: There are always spirit guides and helpers around us, pouring out their love and wisdom. I also came back knowing the immense potential available to each of us within our dreams, and that dreams can be an avenue to travel back to Spirit. My life became a quest to remember who I am, and my explorations into past lives, guides, and dreams have helped me along that path.

My Quest

After I was shot, my youthful ambition to become a scientist was replaced by a yearning to discover why we are here and what our human destiny is. Eventually I went to a Zen Buddhist monastery, where I meditated in stillness for more than two years. I didn't experience any great enlightenment, as I had hoped, but I did discover a lovely place of stillness inside me. This place is called "the silence between thoughts."

I also began to explore nontraditional healing. Conventional medical practitioners had told me that, due to the severity of my injuries, I would be disabled for the rest of what would be a short life. But I knew instinctively that I could heal my body—without their kind of medicine. My spiritual journey toward health and healing led me first to a Hawaiian kahuna, or shaman. This great healer agreed to train me only after discovering that I was of American Indian heritage. She opened the doors of my understanding so that I could see, even more deeply, that Spirit resides in everything and that one can call upon Spirit in times of need. She showed me that life isn't always what it seems, for there is magic in the universe.

I believe that each person is guided to people and situations that will increase understanding and growth. I was also led to a remarkable Japanese woman named Hawayo Takata, a Grand Master of Reiki, which is a method of channeling healing energy from the universe. When we first met, she announced that she had been waiting for me to contact her and asked what had taken me so long! I ended up organizing some of her first courses for Westerners. Hawayo, who was not only my teacher but became a good friend, taught me to access the life force energy in such a way that it would surge down my arms for healing.

Each of my teachers helped me to insert a different piece of my life's puzzle as I began to discover my place in the universe. I also trained with a Shiatsu master, from whom I learned to balance the body by putting pressure on various points that are similar to those used in acupuncture.

Dancing Feather

Of all my teachers, the one who will always have the most sacred place in my heart is Dancing Feather. I was with him as he lay dying in the Santa Fe Indian Hospital, and I remember feeling a very deep sadness over the loss of my good friend and teacher. I was also filled with remorse because I hadn't taken the opportunity to learn more during my apprenticeship with him. I said, "Dancing Feather, what is the most important thing you would have me know?" With a gnarled brown finger he beckoned me to lean closer. As I looked into his fathomless eyes, I felt as if I were falling into the stars. He whispered softly, "Keep it simple," smiled, and fell back against his pillow. And slowly, like a gentle tide coming to shore, the truth of his words sank in. I have never forgotten the wisdom of that statement. Dancing Feather's last words to me were, "Wherever you are, wherever you go . . . I will be there."

I walked out of the hospital with a heavy heart, knowing that I would never see my dear teacher again in this lifetime. I began to cry, at first slowly and softly. Then I looked up at the sky, where dark, formidable clouds were forming. It had been a very dry year, and the crops were suffering from the drought. Suddenly a cool wind came up and huge drops of rain began to soak into the red, parched earth. I cried harder as ragged shafts of lightning tore across the sky. I felt that the spirits of the sky, too, were grieving the loss of my teacher. I began to run. My vision blurred by the pelting rain and my tears, I saw what I thought was an old, drunken Indian slumped on the side of the road. As I passed him he flung up his head as if a steel bar had been pushed up his spine, looked straight at me, and said, "I won't forget." Then he slumped forward again. I couldn't get over how much his eyes looked like Dancing Feather's.

Dancing Feather was a man of few words, but when he did speak, he always spoke the truth. "Wherever you are, wherever you go . . . I will be there." Soon after his death, a peculiar thing began to happen. Whenever I conducted a seminar on healing, people who had the gift of "sight" would say, "I see an Indian standing beside you." And they would describe Dancing

Feather. This surprised me, because at the time I hadn't mentioned him to anyone outside my immediate family. Then feathers began to appear in unusual ways for me and people I came in contact with at important junctures in life.

Feathers

A woman told me this unusual story—only one of many such accounts.

> I am a single mother with three young children. I was going through a very hard time in my life when I couldn't financially or emotionally take care of myself or my kids. I thought they would be better off without me. One morning I arose with a very clear decision to commit suicide that day. I just couldn't go on one more day. Then I heard a knock at my door. I opened it and looked to the right and the left, but there was no one there. Then, just as I was closing the door, I looked down. There, at my doorstep, were three perfectly laid out, shiny, beautiful feathers. As I looked at them, I thought of my three beautiful children—and then I knew I was going to make it. Seeing those three feathers was a turning point for me. I am now financially and emotionally stable and really enjoying my life and my kids.

Again and again I heard stories about feathers appearing. Each feather seemed to have a message. Sometimes it was: "You're doing fine. Just keep going." At other times the message would indicate a direction to take in life. I believe that the feathers carry messages from Spirit, and they are a fulfillment of the covenant that Dancing Feather made on his deathbed.

Many people who have read this book have written to say

that feathers have started appearing in their lives. As you begin to discover who you were in past lives, and to resolve past-life negative programming, feathers may begin to appear to you. By doing the exercises in this book, you begin an incredible journey of self-exploration, and feathers serve as reminders that you are not alone on your journey. There are spirit helpers around you right now, peering over your shoulder, loving you and guiding you. They are helping you remember who you are by facilitating your release of past blockages.

Whenever you see a feather, be still for a moment and listen to your inner voice. It can be a feather that you see on the ground, one that appears in your home, or even one that floats down from the sky. It can be a little feather or a large one. Each feather is a messenger from Spirit. Whenever you see a feather, wherever you are, just stop even if only for a second, and listen for the message. I share with you this gift from my teacher. He would have liked it that way.

My Journey into Healing, Past Lives, and Dreams

After I was shot, not only was I set on a spiritual quest to understand the inner nature of reincarnation, but immediately the door to my dreams flew open. Vivid and sometimes disturbing images flooded me during the night. Sometimes these images seemed so real that the boundaries between waking hours and night hours were blurred. Some dreams were idyllic and even visionary in nature. These dreams were profoundly soothing and reassuring, and occasionally I would even catch a fleeting glimpse of the place to which I had traveled when the doctors thought I was dead. I would clutch at these cloudy images, only to have them vanish like fine mist.

Often, however, my dreams were disturbing. As the nocturnal doors of perception opened for me, I saw images that had been held back for a long time. Numerous images of past lifetimes, seemingly forgotten in the recesses of my mind, began to surge forward, allowing me to experience living in other times and places in history. The onslaught of these images filling my night hours can be likened to a computer downloading information or to a dam whose walls have held back a great river for many years. Through my dreams I began to understand that so many of my beliefs about myself and the world came from my experiences in other lifetimes. By recalling these memories, I was bringing to consciousness old, limiting beliefs, decisions, and judgments that I had carried through lifetime after lifetime. Now I could begin to release them.

There is a psychological adage that says, "To relive is to relieve," and it seemed that these dream images were helping me to relive forgotten experiences so that I could begin to relieve the burden that the past was taking on my life. By exploring my past lives in my dreams, as well as using other techniques, I began to heal, physically and emotionally.

HEALING

As I healed myself from my injuries, people came to me and asked if I could help to heal them as well. I began with hands-on healing. My practice developed very quickly, and I began to work with many people, sharing the methods I had used for my own healing. I developed a natural ability to channel healing energy through my hands, and the results were remarkable.

When a patient came to me for a first treatment, we began by speaking very quietly together. I asked what results the person wanted from the treatment. This helped focus the direction of the healing. I then asked him or her to lie flat on a massage table or a futon. Then I sat next to the patient and became very still. My breathing slowed down. I waited until I felt a warm breeze of energy fill my body. My hands became very warm, almost hot. I then placed my hands very softly on the patient's head until I felt the warm stream of energy within me begin to flow into him or her. I felt a continuous stream of light and sound and love flow through both of us.

Next, I began pushing pressure points on the body; each point corresponded with a different organ or gland. As I applied pressure I would often have powerful experiences, as though I were disappearing into the point. Each point was like an immense tunnel to the stars, and I felt like I was falling through that tunnel into space. The patient seemed to disappear. I disappeared. There were only stars and light and harmonic sound. I found that each point had a different sound and a different color. As I explored my patients' remarkable inner universes, I saw that each point also had a special harmonic or subfrequency. In addition, not only did each point connect with an infinity of inner universes, but there was a direct connection between each point and a specific location, power point, or vortex on the earth, as well as with a specific point in the universe.

Every point that I pushed not only balanced the organs of the physical body while it assisted in the release of negative emotions, it also reached into the innermost and outermost places of their being. I knew that in the still quietness of my healing room, the world was a better place because of what we were doing. Healing energy was radiating from each pressure point on the body to each power point on the planet and into the universe.

Each point synchronized both healer and patient with the

primordial rhythm of the farthest reaches of the galaxy. In those healing sessions I felt very close to the infinite light and love that I had felt in my near-death experience.

It seemed miraculous that with each treatment, not only did my patients greatly benefit, but I was further healed as well. Both healer and patient entered into an exquisite realm of love and healing. I believe that some of the most powerful healing comes when you can step beyond the bounds of separation—when you enter into an exquisite place where bounds diminish. You are no longer the healer, nor is the other person the patient. You are both engaged in a cosmic dance through the stars.

I also began to realize that all my healing work on others was essentially self healing. Each patient was a part of my greater self—something that dwells in all people and all things. Each of my patients was a different aspect of the greater me and represented a particular part of my self that needed help.

For example, at one stage a number of cancer patients came for treatment. As I worked with them I realized that there were a number of similarities between us. Their cancer was eating away at them and, though I didn't physically have cancer, I had some emotional issues that were eating away at me. These issues seemed to transform spontaneously at the same time as my patients experienced positive results from their sessions. I realized that the healing process always began with me. I was never healing anyone but my self.

In my hands-on healing practice I usually had excellent results. Every once in a while, however, I would work with someone whose physical or emotional pain would leave for a time but return later. This was frustrating to me. Realizing that many of our current problems have their source in the past, I began to regress patients to earlier incidents in their lives—often back into early childhood.

PAST LIVES

I often used relaxation techniques to start these regressions. I would ask my patient to lie down and relax as I helped them with breathing techniques and visualization processes. I would then suggest remembering an incident from the previous day. After they had relived this memory, I would suggest going back to a memory from the previous week. I would continue taking them back in time until they arrived at early childhood. In this way my patients were able to recall their buried memories and heal old emotional wounds. I found that many present-day problems were healed by regressing to early childhood and releasing early, negative decisions and beliefs.

For example, a man with a very sore shoulder came to me for hands-on treatment. After I worked on him, the shoulder was fine. However, the pain returned three weeks later, so I regressed him to a time in his childhood when his father had struck him on the shoulder because he felt that his son wasn't meeting his responsibilities. Now, as a grown man, my patient felt he wasn't being responsible enough. He associated feeling irresponsible with having pain in his shoulder. So, whenever he felt irresponsible, he re-created the sore shoulder.

We subconsciously re-create situations in the present that are similar to those in the past. We restimulate the repressed emotions from the past so that we can release them. When my patient regressed to his childhood, he was able to experience the grief and pain and anger that he had suppressed at the time his father struck him. By releasing those emotions, he was able to ease the pain in his shoulder. As children we all made decisions and judgments that continue to influence our present lives. I discovered that helping people regress to the time in their lives when vital negative decisions were made could, more often than not, release those decisions and the corresponding symptoms *forever.*

However, there were a few persistent cases where, even after a regression to childhood, the symptoms returned. I was very puzzled by this. Janet had suffered from ulcers for years. Her doctor had prescribed drugs, a change in her diet, and participation in stress-reduction classes. However, the ulcers persisted. Acting on intuition, she came to me for a treatment. We decided that we might find some clues to her condition in her early childhood. She regressed to the age of twelve, ten, seven, six . . . then suddenly she became very distressed and began to hyperventilate. I told her to watch the childhood circumstances calmly and asked what she was experiencing.

"I've been poisoned!" she said.

"When you were six you had some poison?" I asked.

"No! I've been poisoned!"

I was concerned, thinking that we had uncovered a childhood memory of having been given poison. I asked, "Who is poisoning you?"

"Enemies of my husband are forcing me to take poison."

"Where are you?" I asked, knowing that she wasn't married.

"I'm in India."

At my prompting, Janet proceeded to tell me that she was the young wife of an older man whose very strong political beliefs were in opposition to those of the people in power. She described the anguish she experienced. Though she loved her husband and wanted to support him, at the same time she didn't like the disharmony that his beliefs were causing in their life. One night when her husband was away, his enemies broke into her house and forced her to drink poison. She died feeling helpless and powerless.

I asked her to go back in time into the life that she was seeing and replay it, this time making decisions that would help her feel more in charge of her life and her destiny. She did so, and saw herself actively campaigning to get other people in the village to understand her husband's point of view. She saw people rallying around her husband so that he had a strong platform of support, which provided strength and protection. She saw herself and her husband raising a family, then dying at a ripe old age, well loved in the community. As she described this revised scene, her entire countenance changed and her face shone with a deep peace.

After this session we talked about her present life. She was in a relationship in which she felt helpless; the ulcers had started at about the time that she'd entered into it. We discussed some choices she could make in this relationship. Within a few weeks the ulcers had healed completely, and they didn't return.

Janet's current relationship difficulties had activated memories of similar problems in a past life. In her subconscious, she had equated feeling helpless with poison burning holes in her stomach. Feeling helpless in her current life activated the past-life physical trauma, so she got ulcers that burned holes in her stomach. By changing the images in her subconscious, she was able to change negative programming that was affecting her present life.

When I saw the results in Janet's life I was very excited by the potential of past-life regression. Dealing with problems only in the present can be likened to mowing dandelions. You can cut them down, but they'll keep surfacing again and again. It is by digging down to the roots that you can prevent them from resurfacing. In my therapy practice, when I found a problem that couldn't be solved by exploring early childhood, I would regress the patient to the roots of the problem in a past life. After resolving the past-life issues, the symptoms would almost always disappear permanently.

I found that most of our present blockages can be traced back to a past life. By experiencing what occurred in the past, we can heal physical and emotional problems. With past-life therapy, my patients released ailments and phobias, mended relationship difficulties, increased their creativity, and released blockages to abundance. The results were amazing.

Later, I discovered another technique for tuning in to past lives. When I pushed with my thumbs on a Shiatsu point, often I would see images in my mind. In addition, the person I was working on would often spontaneously see the same images in his or her mind. Sometimes these were images from early childhood that had been forgotten, but more often they were images of past lives.

I began to realize that past-life memories are lodged not only in the brain but in the body, and that stimulating those images for recall had enormous positive results in my patients' lives. I realized that every cell in the body has consciousness, and that each cell holds emotions and past-life memories. I believe that just as DNA has encoded into its structure a blueprint for the physical body, within its intricate structure are memories from this life and past lives! This was an important discovery for the work that I was later to do with group past-life regressions, when I got people to stimulate points on their bodies to help facilitate past-life recall.

Many of my clients began to report that after my treatments their dreams began to change, to feature images and memories of other times in history. It seemed that once the doors to the past opened, dreams became a processing point to release the accumulation of thousands of years of lifetimes that were longing for release.

I was so excited about my clients' results that I began to use past-life regressions in my personal life. At the time I had a weight problem—I weighed more than 170 pounds—and I was constantly dieting. I could lose about ten pounds, but I would inevitably gain it back. When I discovered the power of regression, I took myself back to a time in my childhood. There I saw myself at the age of three being told by my mother what a big girl I was. This was her way of letting me know that I met with her approval. Thus, I equated "big" with "good." As an adult, I naturally wanted to be good, so I was subconsciously helping my body to remain big. Once I had made that realization, I lost fifteen pounds without even trying. But I still didn't weigh what I felt was ideal for me. I kept struggling to meet my weight goal, but without success. At that point, I had another startling revelation in a dream.

My dream was very vivid. Dust assailed my nostrils. Billows of golden dust surrounded the buffalo herd as it stampeded by. Upwind, my nostrils were sensitive to the fetid odor of the fear-filled beasts. I felt rooted to the land, and, strangely, the buffalo charge seemed to reflect the restless stirrings in my soul. Waking up from this dramatic dream, I knew that in my night hours I had been transported over the bridge of time to a past life as a Native American woman. The images and smells in the dream were very real; the shimmering colors very alive. In my waking hours I used that dream as a starting point to regress to a past life where I was a member of a wandering Blackfoot tribe. After having the dream, images and feelings began to fill me spontaneously—even, unexpectedly, during my waking hours. I began to see how many of the habits in my current life could be traced back to my Blackfoot life.

We were a nomadic tribe, always on the move to find enough to eat. In winter there wasn't always enough. Even when there was enough, there was an eating hierarchy. The male elders ate first, then the chiefs and warriors, and finally the young women and children. As an old, physically impaired woman, I was often the last to eat and would go to sleep hungry.

I saw how this past-life experience set in motion a present-day pattern. At mealtimes, in my current life, whenever there was a communal dish rather than individual servings, I felt an intense panic. I was afraid that I wouldn't get enough to eat. Whenever I was served, I would eat voraciously, even if I wasn't hungry. This created physical problems, since I ate so fast that the food wasn't digested properly, and I was also eating more than my body needed. In those moments of panic I was reenacting my memories of not having enough to eat. Experiencing my relationship to food in my life as a Blackfoot Indian helped me understand my present relationship to food. As I released the belief that I wasn't going to get enough, I was able to slow down when I ate and to start eating more in accordance with my body's needs rather than out of an old fear about survival.

In my life as an old Indian woman I developed a hip problem that prevented me from keeping up with the tribe during their moves from camp to camp. It was a tribal tradition to leave the old people behind when they could not keep up. Consciously, as an Indian woman, I understood this: I knew it was necessary to leave the old behind to ensure the survival of the rest of the tribe. However, in that life I subconsciously experienced anguish, loneliness, and the bitterness of betrayal. These feelings were at odds with my acceptance of the ways of the tribe, so I suppressed them.

The images and feelings from my life as a Blackfoot are very clear. After I was abandoned, I found shelter in a small indentation of rock—not quite a cave. The walls felt rough and cold to my touch. The late autumn air was harsh and cold. Each breath of air bit sharply in my nostrils and created an icy burn in my lungs. The cold ripped through my clothes, through my thoughts, through the last vestige of warmth left in me. The sky was a pea-green gray. The snows were late, so there wasn't even the comfort of soft blanketing whiteness to assuage the stark reality of being abandoned. The far black mountains were ragged against the sky. Barren branches were silhouetted against a greasy-gray horizon, punctuating my aching loneliness. It was bitterly cold. My hands were frozen. I couldn't feel my feet. Hunger ate away at my reason. How could they have left me! I'd thought that they were my friends. I'd worked so hard, given much. How could they have left me? I gave up. Let me sleep, I thought. Let me die. Let me die. Let me die . . .

I starved and froze to death with feelings of extreme resentment and loneliness. The feelings and decisions that we have at death are very powerful and often carry forward through many lifetimes. However, it's not *all* the emotions that carry forward. It's the suppressed ones—those we didn't allow ourselves to experience and express at the time—that create present-day blockages.

It wasn't my starving to death that created my weight problem—it was the suppressed emotions that I had carried into my current life. Recalling that Indian memory, I was able to understand why, every time I had tried to diet in this life, I felt incredibly lonely and backed away from the emotional pain. Subconsciously I equated lack of food with being abandoned and lonely. When I allowed myself to experience those painful, suppressed emotions from that former life, I lost the remaining weight I wanted to lose! Furthermore, I have found that past-life therapy is an excellent adjunct to any weight-loss program for people interested in keeping the pounds off. Some 95 percent of those who lose weight through dieting gain it back again. Those who lose weight by going to the emotional source of the problem, which is often in a past life, are usually able to keep it off for good.

Discovering my past life as a Blackfoot Indian enabled me to remove other barriers in my present life. Whenever the tribe moved, we were required to carry heavy things over long distances. In my present life I was always carrying heavy things, often when I didn't need to. Sometimes I would even pick up a heavy stone and carry it for a long distance, for no apparent reason. Not only was this a peculiar habit, but it was damaging my spine. As soon as I recognized where this pattern came from, I no longer felt any compulsion to carry heavy things.

In my life as a Blackfoot woman I was a healer, administering herbs, attending births, and soothing wounds (all things that I have done in this life). Although I was an excellent healer, my hip problem made me feel unworthy of marriage, as I seemed to equate physical ability with worthiness. I never married in that life, and I blamed the tribe for that, thinking it was they who saw me as unworthy.

However, when I was transported into that life as a Blackfoot, I realized that it was not the tribe's judgment but my own that had made me turn suitors away. In my present life, from early childhood I had assumed that I would never marry. Later, my injuries from the shooting made me feel undesirable as a woman, further promoting the idea that I would never marry. Traveling back in time to that point where I made the initial decision as an Indian woman, and reliving it, seemed magically to lift my lifelong blockage to having a fulfilling relationship. I now have a wonderful husband, whom I call the man of my dreams.

So many things in my present life shifted once the door to that Blackfoot life opened. I had always suffered from poor circulation in my feet and hands, even in warm climates like that of Hawaii. This was a legacy from my freezing to death as an Indian. I also found that whenever I got cold, I felt isolated and emotionally numb. I never could understand winter sports such as skiing. It didn't make sense to me that people would *choose* to be cold.

After changing the decisions I had made in that past life, my circulation improved so much that it is now much better than most people's. And I love winter sports. In fact, cross-country skiing is probably about as close as I come to connecting with God. I love the pure white blanket of snow and the stillness of a snow-shrouded forest. It's wonderful to watch the soft crystals float from a high branch when a gentle breeze shakes the tree. I love the swishing cadence of the skis as they glide through the sparkling snow. I would have missed all this joy had I not explored that past life.

Another old pattern that began to dissolve after seeing my Indian life was my strong need to be included in group activities and to get everyone to like me, even if it meant denying what I knew intuitively to be right. I was voted "nicest girl" in high school, which at the time seemed a wonderful honor. Later, however, I recognized what it meant: that I had had to give up so much of my own truth to get everyone to like me. In my subconscious was a core belief that if people liked me, I would survive. When I was dying as an old Indian woman I kept thinking that if my fellow tribe members had liked me more, perhaps I wouldn't have been left behind. So I came into this life thinking I had to get everyone's acceptance. The inner recognition that I didn't have to attain everyone's approval freed me to find my truth. This created an enormous shift in my life.

Each past life contains seeds that sprout in our current lives. Dying cold and hungry and feeling betrayed in my life as a Blackfoot created an emotional charge on betrayal. In my current life I had created situation after situation in which I felt betrayed. In each of these situations I became a whirlpool of emotions—rage, bitterness, resentment, sadness, and grief. In every situation in which I felt betrayed, I later found that I actually had not been betrayed. This was the same pattern that occurred in my life as an Indian. I wasn't betrayed. I knew that if I couldn't keep up I would be left. I knew that this was a tribal law that I adhered to. I wasn't actually betrayed, but I felt that I was. We keep re-creating the same patterns through our various lifetimes until we release them from our personal energy fields. I no longer create situations in which I feel betrayed. But if I did, I feel that I would now be an observer, watching an old pattern unfold rather than being engulfed in the feelings and emotions that used to surround those situations.

After my exploration into my past life as an Indian woman, I began to understand my interest in herbs. I used to own an herb company and often use herbs for healing. I also understood my deep love of nature. I realized why I collected antlers. The Indians used antlers for many things, including tools. Subconsciously I still feel the value of these beautiful creations. I understand my love for the drum and drum rituals. I can trace so many of my present views of life back to my existence as a Blackfoot. Currently I lead ceremonial sessions such as medicine wheel ceremonies, Vision Quests, and sweat lodges, as well as teaching drumming, drum making, and drum painting.

All of this gives me great joy. I have pulled forth what was beautiful and sacred from that past life and incorporated it into my present life. Not only is it valuable to release limiting patterns from the past, but you can also pull out talents and abilities from that time.

I have Indian blood in this life, and I was an Indian in a past life. In my past-life therapy with patients, I find that our present-day heritage can often give clues about past lives. In the past, being an Indian was a hard and difficult life. In my present life I am proud of being Native American. This honoring of my heritage has helped to heal the difficulty I had in the past.

Later, I experienced another past life that was dramatically influencing my present one. For most of my adult life I had struggled with finances and possessions. As soon as I received any money or was given any material object, I seemed to find a reason for giving it away. I had an incessant need to be without possessions and money. Another aspect of this was my choice of clothing: I wore the same style of clothes day in and day out and was reluctant to buy anything new. When I discovered that in one past life I had been a Franciscan monk on a small island off Venice, I understood why I had difficulty creating abundance in this life. I "saw" this life during an experience of déjà vu when I actually visited that island monastery in the early 70s.

As I walked on the beautiful monastery grounds, I spontaneously remembered my life as a monk. It was as if I was transported back through time. I remembered one particular radiant morning, sun pouring through my window and the birds outside chirping a canticle to the cosmos. What a glorious day to be alive! In fact, every day was glorious in the praise of the Lord. My small cell filled with the approaching warmth of the day. I placed my feet on the stone floor. The stones still held some of the coolness of the night and felt smooth and comforting to my bare feet. After my most earnest prayers, though in my heart I was bursting to run, I maintained a restrained decorum in front of the elder brothers as I walked to the garden. I loved working in the garden. The richness of the soil in my hands filled me with contentment and peace. The sound of the birds overhead was like the greatest chorus of angels. A small tendril reaching forth from a dark black seed that I had planted was a most wondrous event. My life was simple, yet filled with a deep, rich peace. I had strong feelings about right and wrong. Money and possessions were wrong. Poverty was good. Poor people were God's chosen. To break any of the commandments was wrong.

Anything that you judge as right or wrong attaches itself to you lifetime after lifetime. In that past life, I had taken vows of poverty and decided that possessions were wrong. In my present life, whenever I was given a present, I felt uncomfortable and anxious and had a compulsion to give it away. My subconscious memories of these monk's vows were influencing my present life to the point where I couldn't allow myself to own anything of value.

The energy from that past life was very strong in my current life. As well as the two years in a Zen monastery, I spent long periods of time in solitude and retreat in my present life. Even when I wasn't living in a monastery, I wore clothing similar to that of the Franciscan monks. Every day I put on a long brown tunic of rough woven cotton over rough brown pants, and large sandals. I wore this outfit to work, at home—even to weddings and other special events. When I released the vows that I made in that past life, I acquired more freedom and abundance in this life.

I realized that material things in themselves are not bad—it is our attachment to or identification with them that creates difficulty. After releasing my vows of poverty, I felt a new freedom to choose what I wanted to have in my life and what I didn't want. I was no longer being controlled by a past decision. I could decide whether or not I wanted to have possessions and do so without feeling guilty. The vows that we make in past lives have an enormous effect on us. It is valuable to recognize and release any limiting vows from past lives that may have a hold on you.

GROUP REGRESSIONS

I was so encouraged by my clients' results and those in my own life that I accepted an offer to teach a course about past lives. I began to do group regressions in these courses and was amazed to see that the same, if not better, results were produced with large groups of people. I worked with between one hundred and nine hundred people at a time, usually averaging around two hundred. I began to notice that over and over again in these large groups, many people would experience past lives in the same country and same period in history. It was as if they had subconsciously decided to come together once again at this exciting juncture to release not only individual karma but collective karma. This idea is based on the theory that you incarnate lifetime after lifetime with the same individuals. These souls can be likened to a flock of birds that migrates to distant countries, yet always flies together. Information gathered in my reincarnation seminars has consistently shown that individuals incarnate in groups and tend to be drawn together lifetime after lifetime.

A striking example of this occurred in Canberra, Australia, a number of years ago. I was giving a past-life seminar that included a regression mediation. During these meditations I don't give any clues that might predispose someone toward a particular past life or a particular time in history. I say only something like, "You are standing in the mists of time, and when the mists lift you will be in one of your past lives." After this process I took a show of hands. It indicated that more than two-thirds of the hundred people in the room felt that during the regression they had experienced a past life in Rome! I had not mentioned Rome before the process. On examination, it seemed plausible that individuals who in a past life had lived in ancient Rome (a planned city that was a center of government, peopled by many government employees) would have chosen to incarnate in Canberra (also a planned city that is a center of government, peopled by many government employees).

At a past-life seminar in Seattle, an inordinate number of people said that they had been World War II fighter pilots; at another seminar, a larger number said that they had been American Pilgrims; at yet another, many had been American Indians. I don't feel that these are coincidences; I believe that, long before this current life, the participants at each seminar made a choice to come together again, as a group, to release limitations from shared past lives.

I received a letter recently from a woman in Germany who had had a remarkable experience while attending a past-life workshop that I had presented in Australia. During my seminars I play music and then ask the participants to walk around the room. I tell them that when the music stops they may very well be standing next to someone whom they knew in a past life. Most people think this is ridiculous but do the exercise anyway. Ursula wrote to say that when the music stopped she was "coincidentally" standing next to another German. There were more than two hundred people in the seminar and she hadn't seen this man before. As they talked, they found that they had been born in the same small village! While she was growing up she had walked past his house every day on her way to school. They had each moved to Canada, to the same town, at approximately the same time—and they had each moved to the same town in Australia at the same time. Now, this could be an amazing coincidence, or it could lend credence to the idea that we are attracted to the same souls lifetime after lifetime. Ursula's letter is not unusual: I have received hundreds of similar ones from people who have attended my reincarnation workshops.

Sometimes at the end of a session I'll ask if there is anyone who wants to describe what they saw during their past-life mediation. At a London seminar, a man said that he had seen himself as an American Indian standing by a cliff; then another Indian came and pushed him over the edge. As he said this, the man sitting next to him (whom he didn't know) went very pale. I asked this man, "What did *you* experience during the past-life process?" He answered in a quavery voice, "I was an American Indian and I was pushing someone off a cliff!" On another occasion a woman said that she remembered a life in nineteenth-century London in which she was in a public park pushing someone in an old wooden wheelchair. The woman next to her looked startled and said that in her meditation she had recalled a life in nineteenth-century London in which she was in a public park being pushed in a wheelchair. One man relived a life in which, as a native of the Amazon jungle, he had helped to destroy an entire neighboring village. The person sitting next to him (a stranger) had experienced watching his Amazon village being wiped out by a neighboring tribe.

I found that in large groups a tremendous energy can be generated that makes it easier for past-life exploration and personal healing. Whenever possible, I work with the energy of the room using ancient clearing techniques [see my book *Sacred*

Space] and I place healers and therapists around the room during regressions to generate healing energy and love so that people's experiences are positive, empowering, and healing. I am now teaching traditional therapists how to incorporate past-life regression techniques into their work. The growing interest in reincarnation by the Western world gives credence to the idea that, as we face the future, there is a collective need to understand where we have come from so that we are better prepared for what lies ahead.

Although there is value in going to a past-life therapist or attending a past-life seminar, you can begin your exploration in your own home, right now, by using the simple exercises described in this book. Many people have reported dynamic positive changes in life by following these simple reincarnation techniques. However, just reading this book, even *without* doing the exercises, can contribute to the healing of unresolved issues from past lives. This occurs because as you focus on understanding your past lives, subconsciously you activate old past-life patterns. This reenactment of past-life situations (which can appear both in your dreams or in the outer circumstance of your life) is both healing and strengthening. There has never been a more powerful time in the evolution of our planet to resolve old issues and negative programming. By focusing on your past life and using the methods in this book, you can heal the past and thus embrace the future with hope and love.

2. REINCARNATION AND KARMA

The concept of reincarnation, the central focus of past-life therapy, has been with us since before recorded history. Current estimates are that more than a third of the people alive today believe that the soul is eternal and returns to earth again and again, through rebirth into new bodies, in order to grow and learn. Each lifetime provides a wealth of experiences that allow each of us as spiritual beings to become stronger, more balanced and more loving, and eventually to reunite with Spirit. (I prefer to use the word Spirit instead of God because some people equate God with a male, judgmental deity in the sky. To me, the words God, the Creator, Great Spirit, Spirit, and cosmic consciousness all mean the same thing, which is the living force within all things.)

Reincarnation experiences can occur in many ways. Have you ever had the eerie experience of being in a strange town and feeling a familiarity almost too deep to describe? Have you heard a particular piece of music and felt transported by it? Or have you ever had a vivid dream about a time in history or a foreign country that seemed extraordinarily familiar and real? All these incidents can have their roots in past lifetimes.

In one life, perhaps you were very poor and thus had a chance to learn humility and resourcefulness. In another, you might have been wealthy in order to learn about dealing with money fairly and positively. You might have been blind in order to learn inner sight, or athletic, in order to experience and understand physical strength. You might have been a woman in one life and a man in another, or Caucasian in one and Asian in another. Try to think of past lives not so much as building blocks but as pieces of a jigsaw puzzle with each piece, or lifetime, making you more knowledgeable and balanced.

Reincarnation and History

Throughout history, great thinkers have pondered the mysteries of life, birth, and rebirth. The earliest record of the theory of reincarnation, which comes from ancient Egypt, says that the soul is immortal and that when the body perishes, the soul enters into another human body. Both ancient and present-day Hindus believe that the soul is immortal and inhabits one body after another in its search for its true divine nature. Centuries before Christ, Buddha taught about the cycle of reincarnation—the great wheel of life and death. Buddhists, like Hindus, strive to be released from the death/rebirth cycle by attaining nirvana, or oneness with God. The Essenes, an early Jewish sect, are also said to have believed in reincarnation.

The Greek philosopher Pythagoras, who lived some five centuries before Christ, not only wrote of reincarnation but described his personal recollections of his various incarnations. His fellow philosopher Plato was also a believer. Napoleon claimed to have been the eighth-century Holy Roman

Emperor Charlemagne in a past life. The French philosopher Voltaire observed that, "It is not more surprising to be born twice than once." The Spanish surrealist painter Salvador Dali said he believed he had been the great Spanish mystic St. John of the Cross. And many famous Americans including Benjamin Franklin, Henry Ford, and Thomas Edison believed in reincarnation.

Reincarnation as a viable personal philosophy is becoming more prevalent in Western culture. Many people find that their spiritual needs aren't being met by current religions or philosophies and are turning instead to the idea of reincarnation. It answers questions such as why we keep repeating the same negative patterns; where our recurring fears and phobias come from; why we feel an instant attraction to some people and some places; and, more important, what our purpose is here on earth. The philosophy of reincarnation allows us to understand the way in which we each weave our own destiny.

Soulmates

One of the most important aspects of life that reincarnation philosophy addresses is that of relationships. Understanding and healing relationship difficulties that have their roots in past lives can help improve the quality of our present relationships. The latter, which are our karmic counterparts, give us the chance to complete unfinished tasks and help us to release negative thoughts and emotions that may intrude into this current lifetime. People with whom we have relationships that originated in a past life are called soulmates.

Have you ever had a brief encounter that left such an intense impression that you could never quite shake off the memory? Many years ago, as I was standing in line to see a film, a tall, serene man emerged from the darkness and walked past me. My breathing stopped, my knees went weak, and I felt I was about to faint. When I turned to look at him, he was gone. Who was this man to whom I had such an extraordinary response? A psychologist might say that I had activated a hidden memory from my childhood of someone who looked like that tall stranger. However, it's very likely that he was a soulmate.

How many times have you caught a brief glimpse of someone across a crowded room and felt an instant rapport, an inner knowingness of a kindred spirit? In that one brief moment, did you feel a yearning to rekindle those memories from the past and hold on to them for an eternity? Or have you ever met someone and instantly felt uncomfortable, confused, and perhaps even angry?

Such meetings are part of a complex web of intrigue that lies deep within our subconscious minds, and that dictates the tapestries of events that weave their way throughout each of our lifetimes. It determines the way we interact with those around us. It also may cause us to feel a deep love or desire for one individual—or hatred, envy, or spite for another. As the soul memories are roused, relationships are rekindled. Almost everyone with whom we connect in this life is likely to have been involved in many of our past lives, perhaps as a brother, sister, parent, colleague, child, or lover.

The effects of past-life experiences are created again in this life. They may be passionate and romantic, adventurous, or angry and vengeful. When we meet again, in this lifetime, it is to relive and rework the relationship. Those familiar eyes across a crowded room are a soul reminder of the individuals with whom we have chosen to interact once again, and the encounter provides us with the opportunity to reexperience those karmic relationships.

The idea of a soulmate usually evokes images of Romeo and Juliet, Tristan and Isolde, or Katharine Hepburn and Spencer Tracy—symbols of a most exquisite love that seems to transcend time and space, with two people finding their perfect complement in each other. Though the term *soulmate* is commonly used to describe the one great love of your life, I believe that soulmates can be defined as *all* the individuals you have been with time after time in past lives and even in other dimensions. This idea is based on the theory that you incarnate time after time with the same individuals. Soulmates tend to incarnate together and are attracted to each other even from the far reaches of the world.

My first understanding of how soulmates are attracted to each other occurred when I was a young college student in the Midwest. I was very much in love with a professor there and we shared a small country home. Sensing that he was seeing another woman, I became distraught, and moved to Hawaii to put the soured love affair behind me. I later moved to a new address in Hawaii. There, over tea with a friendly neighbor, I discovered that she and I had gone to the same university. We even knew some of the same people. As she began talking about a clandestine affair she had had with a college professor, the truth slowly dawned on me—she was the woman with whom my lover had had an affair. Fortunately, the situation was far enough behind us that we could become good friends.

There is a tendency to think that our soulmates are only those individuals with whom we feel an instant affinity. However, in my regression work I have found that soulmates can also be those individuals with whom we experience difficulties in our present lives. In fact, such challenging individuals are often those with whom we have had the most intimate past-life connections.

When soulmates meet, there is usually instant rapport, recognition, or even repulsion. If there was a sexual liaison in a past life, there will likely be a physical attraction in the present life, sometimes an almost explosively intense one. Although soulmates don't always see eye to eye, there is usually a sense of familiarity in the relationship. It is a communication beyond logical explanation, a deep attachment (either negative or positive) that is sometimes telepathic.

Lovemates

One of the deepest mysteries in the philosophy of reincarnation is the idea that every human being has a perfect mate waiting to be discovered. This person has been called a lovemate, dualmate, twin flame, and, most often, a soulmate. Researchers have stated that even in Stone Age religions, one of the main reasons for leading a positive life was so that one could be reborn near his or her perfect loved one in the next life. The eighteenth-century German writer Johann Wolfgang von Goethe wrote a novel based on the medieval idea that couples were divinely united. The novel, *Die Wahlverwandtschaften*, which is usually translated as "Elective Affinities," contends that every individual has a perfect mate waiting to be discovered.

A commonly held theory regarding lovemates is that we were originally androgynous beings—souls that were neither male nor female. Somewhere in time we were split in two; we became either male or female energy—not necessarily male or female bodies. These two halves set forth into the earth plane, a dimension of polarities, to grow and expand, forever striving to reunite. The constant drive toward procreation is seen as a deep spiritual urge for that primal union and for the experience of oneness that occurred before the separation.

Those who hold this theory contend that there will be an increase in the searching for and reuniting with lovemates in the coming years because of the increase in the vibratory rate of the planet. This accounts for the rise in relationships that transcend differences in race, age, gender, religion, and social standing. Some lovemates will be much older or younger than their counterparts, or they will be of different races or socioeconomic standing. Sometimes one or the other lovemate can be in the spirit world rather than in a physical body, giving assistance from the "other side." This can account for the feeling that some loving presence is watching over you. Lovemates can even be the same sex, though one will usually have the negative (feminine) polarity, while the other has the positive (masculine) polarity.

Lovemates don't always have smooth-sailing relationships. In fact, the relationship can be quite stormy, because your lovemate will be your mirror—he or she will emphasize or reflect back to you those aspects of yourself with which you aren't satisfied. For this reason, when lovemates come together, the relationship isn't always enduring. However, when lovemates truly unite, for whatever length of time, there is a true mating of the heart and the soul that is fathomless.

The degree to which you accept and love yourself plays an important role in your success in finding your lovemate. If you feel unworthy of love, when you begin to attract your lovemate, you will think, There must be something wrong with this person if he or she loves me. You will then subconsciously begin to find things wrong with the other person and push him or her away. Your lovemate can even be the person to whom you have been married for twenty years but didn't have the eyes to see.

For many people, the philosophy of reincarnation and soulmates provides an understanding of why we are here. It can give us insight into our current relationships and offer answers to some of life's seemingly unanswerable questions.

The Law of Karma

Intrinsic to the understanding of reincarnation is the understanding of the Oriental concept of karma. "As ye sow, so shall ye reap" is the principle behind the law of karma. It is the fate we create for ourselves as a result of our judgments and our actions in this and in previous lives. Karma is the law of cause and effect—the universal law that determines how each of us may weave his or her own destiny. The idea of karma allows us to understand why one person is dealt adversity all his life while another seemingly has an easy path. In the past, karma was viewed as a kind of cosmic accounting system of debits and credits. It was seen as a punitive and retributive law, especially by Westerners. In the Bible, Job, suffering the loss of his family and his worldly goods, cried out to God, "Teach me and I will hold my tongue and cause me to understand wherein I have erred" (Job 6:24). In the past, karma was believed to mean that all suffering was the result of some previous wrongdoing. Anything negative in one's life was thought to be caused by karma. The handicapped, the incurable, the suffering were all thought to be paying back for some terrible harm that they perpetrated in a past life.

Buddha, however, talked about karma this way: "The end of it is peace and consummation sweet." The Hindus talk about karma as a natural and inevitable consequence of every action.

The idea that karma is God's punitive system is changing now. There isn't a judge in the sky who decides what is right and wrong for each individual. Instead, inside each of us is an inner scale of justice monitoring our integrity. We are our own judge and jury. It is we who are always trying to balance the scales, rather than a stern deity judging us. Our inner scales deem our actions appropriate or inappropriate. The verdict of these inner scales is not always what we *consciously* assume is right at the time, even if it is condoned by religion or society. There are much deeper inner truths to which we adhere, and sometimes they are beyond the rules of society.

I believe that we create not only our reality but our karma. For example, if you cheated someone in a past life and you have not understood or made peace with this event, then you may feel unworthy and deserving of punishment. So, in your present life you create difficult situations around yourself and find yourself being cheated. I don't believe that there is a cosmic punishment—only self-punishment. The extent to which you can shift your core beliefs about yourself and the world around you is the extent to which you can step beyond karma.

THE NATIVE AMERICAN VIEW OF KARMA

The American Indians' view of karma was slightly different from that of other Westerners or even the Eastern view. Conscious acts in life were made by Native Americans with the understanding of how those acts would affect the entire tribe and the following seven generations. For example, if they wanted to cut down a tree, they would think about how that would affect the following seven generations. In some tribes, inappropriate acts were not physically punished; instead, the offender would take part in numerous discussions with tribal elders until the full consequences of his or her act were understood.

Native Americans believed that each and every action affected the whole of life. They intuitively understood that all life and all actions are connected, that we live in a viable, pulsating, living universe, and that all life is interrelated and interconnecting. The flutter of a butterfly's wings in the Rocky Mountains affects the tornadoes of the Philippines, which affect a baby suckling its mother in a small village in Italy.

Those ancient native people understood that every act has consequences. This law applies to the physical world as well as to the ways of man: Newton's third law of motion states that every action has its reaction, which is equal and opposite. In the realm of karma, the power of our thoughts is remarkable. Every thought has a life of its own—has form and substance in the causal world. Depending on the intensity, passion, and clarity of the mind of the thinker, every thought creates ripples in the energy field of the planet. Actions and words create waves of energy that echo throughout the universe. In this way we are constantly creating and balancing karma.

MANIFESTATIONS OF KARMA

Karma can manifest itself in different ways. First, it can manifest symbolically. People who in a past life were never willing to see the truth about themselves and the world around them might be born physically blind in order to learn to perceive truth through intuition and feeling. Someone who, as a Viking warrior, cruelly shed much blood in battle might develop anemia. I had a young client who could not swallow very easily; through regression, we discovered that in a past life as a dancer, she was forced into a situation that she couldn't "swallow."

Karma can also be a means of balancing the scales. For example, a woman who had been a lady-in-waiting during the Renaissance always sped through relationships in that life without taking the time to listen to others. In this life, she feels that no one ever listens to her.

Some afflictions and difficulties don't necessarily come into the "symbolic" or "scale-balancing" categories. For example, someone with a physical affliction might incarnate to be of service to other people. A child born with Down's syndrome might be a very evolved being who has incarnated to allow others to experience the gift of giving.

I'm sometimes asked about karma associated with that most devastating event, the death of a child. I believe that karmically there are two reasons why a child might die young. The first is that the child came in service to his or her family and friends. When a child dies, everyone touched by the death usually undergoes an enormous amount of soul-searching and a shift of consciousness. Though incredibly painful, this process usually promotes spiritual growth. The second reason, I believe, is that the child who dies is an evolved soul that doesn't need a very long lifetime. He or she needs just a short period of physical existence to round off their earth-plane experiences. I believe that a soul contract is made with the parents and other family members before the spirit incarnates. Although much pain ensues, powerful spiritual growth arises from this extremely difficult experience.

INSTANT KARMA

Be aware of what you judge in others. Often the very thing that you judge in them will become a part of your life until you accept and forgive the foibles of others. I'll give a very simple example. One day in a grocery store I heard a mother shouting angrily at her young child. I found this very upsetting and thought she was wrong to shout at her child like that. I might have even given her a look that said, What you are doing is bad! Several weeks later, I was out shopping and my young daughter was driving me to distraction. I found myself yelling at her. Then suddenly I stopped—in that moment, I was filled with deep compassion for that other mother. The world is an infinitely better place when we don't judge the actions of others. The Indians would say: "Walk a mile in my moccasins."

As life on our planet continues to speed up, we will find ourselves balancing the karmic scales faster. I call this "instant karma." For example, if you judge someone for being inarticulate, the next day you may find yourself in a situation where you feel inarticulate. It is not a punishment, but rather your way of creating a circumstance that will allow you to be more understanding and less judgmental of others. And it will happen faster and faster in the years ahead as there is an increasing momentum toward completion. You will find instant karma occurring more often. It's a way of measuring how fast you are growing spiritually. The speedier your growth, the more quickly your thoughts will manifest and your judgments will return to you. Uncompleted relationships and unfinished business of the past, both in this life and in past lives, will move to the forefront for long-awaited completion.

I believe that, because of this hastening, many people are going through more than one lifetime within this evolutionary cycle. Many people do not want to take the time to reincarnate and grow up to fulfill the karma of just one particular lifetime. They have so much more that they want to complete. Many are going through several lifetimes during their present one. In the past, an individual might have been born in a certain village, worked at the same occupation as his father and his father before him, married and died—all in the same village. Now, someone might spend half of his or her life working as a cook in Brazil and the second half working as a psychologist in Greece. Each half of the life could have an entirely different agenda, and could fulfill completely different karma.

In any discussion of karma it is important to discuss the view that holds: "I can't do anything about it. It's my karma." No matter how difficult the situation in which you are involved, no matter what difficulties life has dealt you, you are not stuck with your situation. You have free will to change your circumstances or the way in which you view them. Your karma hasn't stuck you in unalterable situations. The past, present, and future are changeable. You *can* change your karma and your resulting life circumstances.

Destiny and Free Will

I believe that each of us is born with a predestined future. I believe that on the day we are born, our date of death has already been decreed. My father's mother was an astrologer who had trained with a remarkable man named Manly Hall. She said she had seen a predilection toward her own death in her astrological chart, and I don't think she was surprised when her time came to leave her body.

However, as fervently as I believe in predestination, I also believe in free will. I do not have difficulty in holding two seemingly opposed points of view. In fact, I believe that the more opposing points of view you can hold, the more evolved a human being you are. I believe that beyond linear time there is a changeable future *and past*, and that it is possible to shift consciousness so that you can choose an entirely different timeline with a new subsequent past and future. In other words, you are not stuck with your past, and your future is malleable. (See chapter 9 for more on future lives.)

In the book *Autobiography of a Yogi*, Paramahansa Yogananda writes about astrology and karma. He states that one's astrological chart can show all the past karma that one has accrued, lifetime after lifetime. He writes: "A child is born on that day and at that hour when the celestial rays are in mathematical harmony with his individual karma." He also states that through prayer, spiritual practices, and right conduct you can convert difficult karma that might have brought the "thrust of a sword" to become only the "thrust of a pin." However, Yogananda warns that those astrologers who can accurately decipher your karma from your astrological chart "are few."

Not long ago I had some remarkable experiences that make a very solid case for predestination. I was in southern Africa conducting seminars and meeting members of the Zulu tribe. In the course of my travels I met a very special Dutch woman. I was due to go to Holland immediately afterward and she said that since she, too, was going to be there at the same time, she would like to cook dinner for me.

It was a warm afternoon when I climbed up the narrow stairs in Holland on the appointed day. The sitting-room window was open to the canal below and the small room was filled with sounds from the street. I heard the metallic sounds of bicycles and the quiet murmurs of conversation from a nearby cafe. Sun reflecting off the canal flooded the room with golden light. Then my new friend began to bring in tray after tray of food. Each bite was filled with magic—the colors, smells, and textures all blended together in a rich gastronomic tapestry. When we had finished, she said, "Denise, there is a story I would like to tell you. It is a true story."

She talked about having spent time in India. During her visits there she heard of a remarkable place in the distant mountains where families descended from a famous astrologer had kept his records for hundreds of years. When the records became faded, they were meticulously copied.

During this astrologer's lifetime, whenever someone consulted him for an astrological reading, not only did he do their current chart, but he also drew up charts for their *future* lifetimes! So, if you were lucky enough to have been one of his original clients, hundreds of years ago, you could have had the chart for your present life drawn up—hundreds of years in the future. He told his clients that if they came to retrieve their records in their future lives it would be valuable for them.

At first I thought this sounded almost too amazing to be true. I thought perhaps the legend was a ruse to make money, so that members of a poor village could earn a living. When I voiced these thoughts, however, I was told that not only was no one ever charged for the charts but that visitors weren't even allowed to present flowers or gifts.

She decided to travel to the mountains with a friend. When she arrived, she told the villagers her birthday and her place of birth. They searched but were not able to find her chart. Therefore, they didn't think that she was one of the people who had had their charts prepared hundreds of years before. They did, however, find her friend's chart.

In her friend's present life he had a very painful skin condition. In his chart it said that during his incarnation in the twentieth century he would have a skin condition because he had not been kind to lepers in a previous life. The chart said that to get rid of the skin condition he must give charitably to leper patients. When he returned home from India, he donated money to charities connected with leprosy, and his skin condition completely cleared up. When eventually he stopped giving to those charities, his skin problem returned.

I would have regarded this as no more than an interesting story, except that only a month later I heard a similar tale. I was in London giving a series of lectures on reincarnation when I was asked to take part in a BBC radio program in which guests from different backgrounds participated in lively discussions of varied topics. One of the other guests was a man who originally came from India. At the end of the show this very soft-spoken Indian gentleman, a doctor and sculptor, said, "There is something that I would like to show you."

As we sat in the studio lobby he pulled out a sheaf of faded papers torn at the edges. The pages were covered in what I assumed was the ancient Sanskrit language. The doctor then proceeded to tell me that when he was nineteen, he had traveled with his father to a place where astrological records had been kept for hundreds of years. It sounded like the same place that had been described to me by the Dutch woman. After a very long and arduous journey, the doctor and his father arrived on a rainy day—a very unusual occurrence in that part of the world. They located the astrological charts for their present lives and found that both had indeed been clients of the famous astrologer hundreds of years before. The doctor told me that his chart said that he would come to claim his records when he was nineteen, and on a rainy day. His chart also correctly gave his name in his present life. As we looked over his well-worn chart, I said, "You've had this chart for some thirty years. Has it been accurate?" He went carefully through the chart with me (though I had only his word for what it said, as I cannot read Sanskrit) and showed me many examples of where it had been accurate.

I pass these stories along to you as they were shared with me. I found both individuals to be very honest, trustworthy people. I believe them and their accounts.

Transmigration

I'm often asked if we have always been human beings in past lives. I have found that it is not unusual for individuals spontaneously to remember a lifetime as an animal. This is especially true if they came from cultures where the predominant religious belief is based on reincarnation and the transmigration of souls into animal bodies. It is also true for people who come from earth-based cultures. I have found it very unusual for someone from our Western culture to recall a life as an animal in a past-life regression. I don't think this means that Westerners haven't had animal lives whereas people from native cultures have. Rather, I believe that, since they live closer to the earth, native peoples are more in tune with nature and so are more likely to *remember* past lives as animals.

Let me tell you a true story that gives credence to humans having had past lives as animals. My years in the Zen Buddhist monastery were very austere. We were required to sit in meditation in the lotus or half-lotus position for up to sixteen hours a day. During meditation we sat facing a bare wall inside the monastery. We weren't allowed to have our eyes open, for the Zen masters felt that we might be tempted to look around. We weren't allowed to close our eyes, either, for they felt that we might fall asleep or start visualizing instead of meditating. Instead, we were required to keep our eyes half-open in an unfocused gaze at the wall. When we sat, our backs had to be ramrod straight, and we weren't allowed to move.

In these circumstances it was easy to be distracted by pain or tiredness. So, as an act of compassion, with lightning accuracy the Zen master would strike the shoulder of a Zen practitioner with a *kyôsaku* stick to ensure attentiveness in his discipline. A *kyôsaku* stick is similar to a flat baseball bat. The catch-22 of this practice was that if the Zen master deemed that you were doing well, he would smack just as hard in order to encourage you!

In the quiet of the monastery, inner demons from our subconscious or from our past would rise into our awareness. This was disturbing and often took great courage to face. We were told by the Zen masters that no matter what we saw or experienced during our meditation, it was all an illusion. We were told to detach ourselves from it. I don't know if this is the best psychological way to deal with emotional difficulties, but this was the way it was done in the Zen Buddhist tradition for hundreds of years, so we accepted it.

One of the most avid of my fellow Zen students was a man named Chuck. One day, perhaps overwhelmed by the difficulty of the monastic practices, he committed suicide. While living at the monastery I had adopted a stray white cat, which shortly after Chuck's death had six pure white kittens. One of the kittens had one blue eye and one green eye. *Chuck had had one blue eye and one green eye.* One day this kitten fell off the top of the garage, injured a leg, and began to walk with a limp. *Chuck had walked with a limp.* When all the kittens were old enough to be out chasing butterflies and scampering through the monastery gardens, we noticed something very unusual. Every time the gong was sounded to begin meditation, the kitten with the two different-colored eyes would run to the door nearest the meditation room. (Cats were not allowed inside the monastery.) This very solemn kitten would sit absolutely still outside the door for the entire, lengthy meditation. This occurred day after day and seemed very unusual for a young kitten, which one would have expected to be active and playful. We couldn't help but wonder if that kitten had been our friend Chuck. The kitten did seem very attentive whenever we talked to her, and she particularly responded to the name that we gave her—Chuckee.

Chuck had been a very enlightened man, so perhaps after his death he didn't want to take the time to incarnate into a human body and go through all the effort of growing up. Perhaps he came back in the cat's body to experience just a little of the physical world before going on to the next stage of his development.

Whether you have had a past life as an animal or in an exhulted position or in deep despair, when you can view your past lives in the larger context of reincarnation and karma, the many pieces of the puzzle as to why you are here on earth at this time in history, and what your purpose is, will begin to fall into place.

3. PAST-LIFE THERAPY

There are documented cases of convincing detail being recalled during past-life regressions that are later validated through historical research. You do not have to believe in reincarnation for past-life therapy to be beneficial in your life. Many of my clients didn't believe in reincarnation, yet they gained immense value from the therapy. When a person's life changes as a result of experiencing images in his or her mind, true healing has occurred. Even if the images that come to the surface are not past-life memories but are simply symbols of the subconscious, they deserve to be heard. They are legitimate expressions of our inner being and can expand the quality of our lives.

Past-life therapy can sometimes give answers that neither traditional medicine nor traditional therapy provides. Of course, there can be many contributing reasons for our problems in life, and it can be all too easy to blame these on past-life behavior. Nevertheless, past-life exploration has proved incredibly powerful in many cases where other types of therapy have failed. Through understanding what we have been in previous lives, we can better understand our place and mission in the present. Life is not a one-time affair; nor is it a series of meaningless experiences strung together. Past-life exploration can assist the process of gradually realizing our full potential as conscious, loving beings.

Health

Past-life therapy can have a positive effect on all aspects of life and is especially beneficial for health problems. Karen was a client who came to me because she thought she was sabotaging herself in her desire for a long-term, loving relationship; she also felt that she had a weight problem. Although there is not necessarily a connection between weight and relationships, Karen felt there was for her. She was a thirtyish well-dressed woman, about thirty pounds overweight. She was certain that her size was preventing her from experiencing a long-term, satisfying relationship.

In her past-life therapy she vividly remembered a life as a prostitute in eighteenth-century England. She recalled the bitter cold of the London streets, the occasional frantic encounters with customers, and the long, hungry days. She was very unhappy in that life. During regression she relived her grief at being stuck in a profession that she considered harmful to her. In addition, she got in touch with a belief that she had formed at the time: "If I'm attractive, men will desire me for my body, and I will feel cheap and degraded." She came into her current life with that belief embedded in her "bioenergy matrix." This is your personal energy field, which is made up of all the different aspects of your other energy fields, such as your emotional body, your astral body, your etheric body, and your bioelectrical system (this is the meridian system that acupuncture works on). Beliefs, decisions, and judgments are not just lodged in your brain but in your physical body and in the myriad energy fields that surround and penetrate your body.

In her regression, Karen discovered that even though consciously she wanted to feel attractive and desired, subconsciously she was afraid that she would be degraded again. This core belief had been controlling her life since she was a child. Anytime a man was attracted to her, she would subconsciously sabotage any chance of a relationship.

During the regression she was able to release her old belief, and her entire life changed as a result. She embraced a new belief about herself: "I can feel and be attractive. People are attracted to me for who I am. Who I am is special." Almost immediately she started to lose those thirty pounds, but, more important, she began to feel good about herself. Karen is now happily married and looking and feeling attractive. (See chapter 6 for past-life resolution techniques.)

A young man named John came to me for a regression to treat a physical problem he'd had for many years: He couldn't perspire—his sweat glands didn't work. His skin was dry, and he was very uncomfortable. He had tried numerous medications, to no avail. He regressed to a time when he had been a servant at a Russian court. There, he was required to stand at attention for hours during banquets in case guests wanted anything. During one important banquet he had a very full bladder, but he wasn't allowed to leave his post. Eventually he lost control and ran out of the banquet hall. In a subsequent fit of anger, his master killed him.

In the regression John discovered a subconscious belief that he should hold back his body excretions or he would die. His body translated this idea in such a way that he stopped perspiring. As soon as he discovered the source of his difficulty and resolved it, immediately (during the session) his sweat glands began to work. They have continued to do so ever since.

Relationships

Past-life regression can also help us understand relationships. A daughter who resents her mother telling her what to do may find that in a past life their roles were reversed: the present daughter was the mother, and her mother the child. The present daughter may never have gotten over the feeling that *she* should be in charge, not the other way around. Remembering and understanding why she feels the way she does about her mother can help her to create a healthier relationship in which she is not being run by her past programming.

Sue had worked at the same job for seven years. Almost every day she was angry with her boss. He noticed every detail of her work, and she felt that he was suffocating her. In her regression she discovered a past life in which her current boss had been her husband—and he had not been attentive at all. They had been pioneers in Montana in the 1800s and had lived in a small mountain cabin miles from any other habitation. In that life as a pioneer wife, Sue was very lonely and wanted company. Her husband used to leave their cabin, sometimes for weeks at a time, to go hunting and exploring. She used to complain that he wasn't attentive enough. On one occasion when he was away, Sue was caught in a landslide behind the cabin and suffocated to death.

When Sue realized that her present boss was trying to make up for being inattentive in their past life, she forgave him (while she was regressed) for not being attentive to her. She also let him know it wasn't his fault that she had suffocated. Even though she never told her boss about her regression, she said that from that day forward he seemed completely changed. Even the other office workers noticed the difference. He was much more at ease with her, and everyone in the office enjoyed the benefits of his more relaxed mood.

Abundance

Whenever Mark started to get ahead financially, he would back down from his success. He was never quite able to make ends meet for his family. A common expression of Mark's was, "We are poor but we are happy." In a regression, he saw that he had been a wealthy landowner in the Middle Ages. His family had been taken and held for ransom by marauding bandits. He never saw his young wife (who happened to be his wife in this life) again in that life.

He recalled night after night, slouched in damp quarters in his manor house, blaming himself and his wealth for the loss of his wife. This subconscious guilt had carried forward into his present life: He felt that if he had too much money, his family would be taken from him. This feeling was so strong that, had he ever made enough money, he would likely have separated from his family to support his subconscious belief. After Mark recognized this belief pattern, a remarkable financial change occurred. He was quickly given a promotion, as he was no longer sabotaging his advancement, and, interestingly, he went into real estate. He and his family are now quite prosperous.

Activating Talents and Abilities

An exciting area of regression is the activation of past-life talents and abilities for use in the present life. Rob came to one of my seminars and regressed to a time when he had played the violin. The following week he bought a violin and began taking lessons. He reported that his teacher was astounded at how quickly and easily he was able to learn.

Carolyn had always wanted to sing but felt that she didn't have a very good voice—she said people used to tease her about it. After she experienced a past life in which she had been an excellent singer, she said that it seemed almost magical how quickly her voice had improved. Now she sings in a choir in her hometown.

In my seminars I often do a process specifically aimed at activating talents, abilities, and other qualities from past lives. At the end of one of these processes a woman came up to me and said, "I don't understand. In my past-life experience I saw that I was a shepherd. All I did every day was spend time in the hills by myself, occasionally herding sheep. What talent or ability is that?"

"Tell me about your present life," I said.

"Well, I'm pretty busy in my life because I have six kids." She had activated a life in which she had experienced tremendous peace. I believe she tuned in to that particular life so that she could bring some of that peace into her present, hectic life.

I've developed a technique in my seminars that seems to help bring a particular talent or ability into the present life. While the participants are in a state of altered consciousness, with their eyes closed, experiencing a talented past life, I ask them to move or position their body as if they were participating in their particular talent. For example, when Rob recalled a life as a violinist while his eyes were closed, I asked him to stand up and move his arms and body just as if he were playing a violin. In this way he began to understand what it feels like to play the violin. This process helps the body remember how to do the particular activity. Moving your body while experiencing a past life actually helps to "implant" that special quality into your present physical body.

In one seminar when I was leading this talent process I saw a young man in the corner of the hall doing what looked like push-ups. I assumed that he must have been a very good athlete in another life and was doing push-ups to bring his past athletic abilities into the present. During the break I asked him what past-life talent he had encountered. His face turned red as he lowered his voice and whispered, "I was a great lover!" I can only hope that his lovemaking abilities have improved as a result of his sojourn into the past.

Releasing the Fear of Death

Another benefit of past-life regression is the release of the fear of death, which enables you to live much more fully and intensely. When you really experience the fact that you are infinite and eternal, and that *you* don't die when your body dies, you begin to feel a deep inner peace that pervades your everyday activities. The thought of dying can be frightening or extremely sad to someone who thinks that this one life is all there is.

Mitchell had AIDS. He had never had very strong religious beliefs, and was terrified of dying. He didn't believe in reincarnation, but a friend persuaded him to consult me. I told him that he didn't have to believe in reincarnation—instead, we could do a past-life process and call the images he saw "soul dramas." I explained that the images he would experience were a valid expression of his subconscious mind, and that whether they were past lives or symbolic expressions of his inner psyche wasn't important—those inner messages deserved to be heard no matter where they came from. He could accept that point of view. (*Soul dramas*, incidentally, is a term originated by my friend Roger Woolger, an excellent past-life therapist and writer on the subject.)

Mitchell very quickly went into a deeply relaxed state. The images and feelings of other times and other places came very easily to him. Suddenly he had a spontaneous experience seemingly unsolicited by anything I said. He said that he saw all the bodies that he had ever inhabited in all of his lifetimes coming forward like a great gathering of friends. Some were male, some were female. Many different races were represented. As he stood in the center of this gathering, one by one these past selves came forward and told him what he had gained from each life. Finally, the body that looked exactly like his present one came forward and said, "Each life allows you a greater and deeper understanding of who you are in your entirety. Each life is special, important, and valuable. The body and the life that you are currently inhabiting is allowing you to develop your ability to receive love. You are learning this lesson well, and soon you will be going home." At this point Mitchell began to sob. It seemed that a dam of uncertainty, fear, and pain was released as he cried. When he stopped, he smiled and said, "I have never felt such a deep sense of peace. I am ready to go when it is my time." He died a few weeks later, but I was told that his last few weeks of life were filled with a profound grace and peace.

Why Past-Life Therapy Works

It is important to understand why using past-life therapy is so healing. It works because it allows you to get to the source of your problem; until then, you are dealing with symptoms rather than causes. Many of our compulsions and phobias are rooted in the distant past. For example, if you have always hated wearing anything tight around your neck, you may discover a lifetime in which you were choked to death. By recognizing and experiencing your past memories and associated emotions, your present life behavior frequently changes.

We often create present-day incidents that subconsciously remind us of past-life experiences as a way to heal the original pain. If emotions such as fear, anger, or grief are suppressed during traumatic events in a past life, they stay in our energy fields and form inner conflicts that recur lifetime after lifetime. We continue to push these undesired feelings from the past deeper into our psyches, building a greater and greater barrier between ourselves and whatever we are afraid to feel. When you reexperience a past-life incident, the emotions and decisions that were suppressed for so long have the opportunity to come to the surface and release themselves, so that they no longer control you.

To understand why past-life therapy works, it's important to understand that it is not necessarily the trauma and the emotions that you experienced in your past lives that create problems in your present life. Rather, it is the trauma and emotions that you *suppressed* in the past that create difficulties in the present. Your past-life experiences do not necessarily create continuing problems—it is your *reactions* to those experiences and your blocked emotions that create the havoc. For example, merely having fallen down a ravine in a past life won't necessarily create a blockage in your present life, but having fallen while feeling emotional anguish can.

Joshua experienced a past life as a young man in medieval Europe. He remembered telling his trusted friends at the time that, contrary to the accepted belief, he thought that the king wasn't directly descended from God. His friends were furious and chased him, causing him to fall down a ravine. As he fell, he was in a turmoil. He loved his friends, yet his feelings of love were at odds with his fear of them while they chased him. As he fell, he made a decision that he would never again share his feelings honestly.

In Joshua's present life he had always been afraid to speak his mind. In fact, often when he began to say what he really felt, he physically tripped and fell. Joshua had a subconscious association between speaking his mind and falling. It wasn't the physical trauma of falling in a past life that caused his present-day blockages—it was the suppressed emotions at the time that he fell. Joshua was able to change his lifelong pattern by using the past-life resolution techniques in chapter 6, and says that he now feels very confident in his life. He can now communicate what he really feels without fear.

Imagine two similar scenarios. In the first, a young Aztec warrior is fighting alongside his best friend. The dust is churning. Spears are flying on either side of the gallant warrior. Suddenly in the haze of battle a spear comes straight at the chest of the friend. The young warrior steps in front of the spear, valiantly saving the life of his friend. Mortally wounded by the spear thrust to his chest, as he dies he feels a deep peace, for he has saved his friend's life.

In the second scenario, two young warriors are battling side by side. They are best friends. Suddenly, in the thrall of battle, obscured by thick haze and dust, one turns to the other and thrusts a spear into his chest. As the warrior lies dying on the battlefield, he learns that his best friend is having an affair with his wife and wants him out of the way. He dies making a decision that he can never really trust anyone.

In both scenarios the physical trauma is the same—death is

caused by a spear wound to the chest. However, in the first instance the Aztec warrior feels exhilaration at having saved the life of his friend. In the second scenario, however, he decides it's not safe to trust anyone. In future lives, whenever he begins to get close to someone, similar memories and decisions are activated. Whenever he begins to trust someone, he experiences severe chest pains and a fear of being betrayed. For him, getting close to someone activates an emotional and physical response from a past life.

The Role of the Subconscious in Past-Life Therapy

"You are what you think." This refers not simply to what you *know* you think, but to what you *don't know* you think. For example, you may be unaware that deep inside your subconscious lie fears and beliefs that you are perhaps unworthy and don't deserve success in life. These fears and beliefs set up inner blocks to fulfillment and create frustration in life. There's a good reason for this. Your subconscious mind exerts a far greater control over your life than you can possibly realize. It literally directs your reality. Imagine a plane flying straight toward a mountainside in the fog. The control tower (the conscious mind) can be yelling: "Turn back! Turn back!" But unless the subconscious mind (the pilot) gets the message, the plane will crash into the mountain.

People often wonder why the subconscious accepts self-defeating programming in the first place. After all, don't we want the very best for ourselves? Don't we all really want to be healthy, happy, and successful? The answers to these questions lie in the nature of the subconscious mind. Although your conscious mind has the ability to reason and decide what is best for you, it cannot implement any decision unless the subconscious mind agrees. An alcoholic may consciously want to give up drinking, yet he will continue to drink despite his conscious mind's desperate desire to stop. The subconscious acts as it has been programmed to act, in much the same way as a computer is programmed.

For example, a mother might say to her small child, "You're so clumsy. You have no rhythm. You'll never be able to dance." The child's critical faculties are not developed enough to reject this negative programming, so she may grow up being very clumsy and having no sense of rhythm because her subconscious has accepted the idea of clumsiness. In other words, clumsiness has been programmed into the subconscious. This idea then becomes an integral part of the child's view of herself. As an adult she might reason that she doesn't need to be clumsy and with enough training will be able to dance. However, if the conscious mind proposes a belief that is different from the subconscious programming, the subconscious mind will be the dominant one.

The subconscious mind is also of great importance to our survival. For example, if you were bitten by a barking dog when you were four years old, your subconscious mind probably programmed a fear of barking dogs. As an adult, if you came upon a barking dog—even a very small dog tied with a heavy chain—you would likely feel momentary fear, because the fear of barking dogs had been programmed into your subconscious mind to protect you—to ensure your survival. Your conscious mind may know that you are safe, but the programming is so strongly embedded in the subconscious that you react with fear.

Your subconscious mind accepts programming not only from early childhood but from past lives. For example, I had a client who was so terrified of bees that she became almost paralyzed whenever she saw one. She had been stung to death by bees in a past life, so her subconscious mind, wanting to ensure her survival, made a decision to stay away from bees. Even though the conscious mind says, "It's just a little bee. You are much bigger and stronger," the subconscious mind takes precedence.

The subconscious mind is so powerful that beliefs from early childhood and past lives become "glued" into your energy field and coalesce into form in the physical world. For example, if you have a core belief that all your romantic relationships will fail, you will continue to create relationships that fail—even though consciously you want to be in a long-lasting, loving relationship. Past-life therapy works by reaching deep into the subconscious mind and literally reprogramming the old beliefs and decisions that are influencing every aspect of your life. (See chapter 6 for past-life resolution techniques.)

No Victims—Just Volunteers

It's important to remember that when you connect with a past life, either through your dreams or in waking consciousness, there are no victims—just volunteers. Every experience you have had was necessary for your growth and to get you to the point at which you are now. As uncomfortable as this may make you feel, every lie you ever told and every nasty thing that you did or that was done to you was necessary for your learning. Remember this if you regress to a lifetime in which you were either a victim or a tyrant.

I imagine the victim-volunteer scenario going something like this: You are walking around in the spirit world. You've examined your past lives and decide that for your next incarnation, it would be valuable for your evolution as a human being to learn some humility. You begin to grab passing spirits. "Hey, I'm about to incarnate. Why don't you incarnate too and teach me some humility?" The spirits all shy away from you, saying, "No way! I'm not going to mess up my karmic evolution by teaching you humility."

Then finally shuffling up to the Pearly Gates comes Harry, an old acquaintance. Harry is someone with whom you have shared lifetime after lifetime—someone you love deeply on a soul level. "Hey, Harry, I really need to learn humility. How about it?" And Harry shrugs, lovingly puts his arm around you, and agrees.

Those individuals who victimized you the most are the very ones who love you the most deeply on a soul level. In my regression work I have discovered, time and time again, that after processing the grief and rage and bitterness that we hold toward our victimizers, there is almost always an enormous well of love.

Forgiving Past-Life Circumstances

One of the most powerful things that you can gain from past-life therapy is forgiveness. Often, to be able to heal, you must be willing to forgive the past. It is much easier to forgive those who have hurt you in your present life when you understand the karma that precipitated the situation. When you travel to the past-life source of your hurt and forgive yourself and others, a loving energy weaves its way through time and space to your present life. It goes without saying that it is important to forgive those who hurt or denied you in a past life; however, it is just as important to forgive yourself for those things that you did to others. (If you have difficulty letting go and forgiving, you must forgive yourself for not forgiving.)

Often, when people have regressed to a past life, they reach a space beyond forgiveness—a space where they realize that everything that ever happened to them was necessary for growth and development. In fact, without those experiences they would not be who they are today. The plane beyond forgiveness is acceptance—total, unconditional acceptance, without judging yourself or anyone else. I find this one of the most healing aspects of past-life therapy.

I am often asked if my past-life explorations have allowed me to discover why I was so brutally shot. Yes, I have found some satisfactory answers. Using past-life exploration, I came to understand my karmic connection with my attacker, and this helped me to forgive him. I shared a life in China with him. All the people in our small village lived in houses that were built up off the ground. The villagers placed bodily wastes through holes in the floor into containers underneath the houses. Every morning, a man (the one who shot me) came and cleared away the waste from beneath the houses. This man was more or less an "untouchable," with no social standing in the community. Though my disdain for him in that life was a minor thing to me, it was major to him. Just as in this life, shooting me was only a matter of slight concern for him (it is believed that he had killed a number of people), it was a major concern for me. We had a slight yet intense karmic connection. I had never seen him in my present life before I was shot, and I saw him only once, at the trial, after I was shot.

When I realized my past-life connection with this man, I finally understood why my last thought before I was hit was: He's aiming too low! I had a subconscious desire to balance the karma of having treated him cruelly in that past life. (If he had aimed any higher, he would have killed me.) Through discovering my past connection with this individual, I was able to forgive him and accept what had happened, thus releasing any resentment that could be carried into my present relationships.

Some of the most rewarding comments I get after past-life seminars relate to forgiving present- and past-life circumstances. In Australia I conducted a past-life process in a seminar at the Japanese-owned Nikko Hotel. A woman who attended that seminar later wrote me an interesting letter saying that on entering the hotel, an intense wave of resentment and panic had come over her. She thought, "I can't attend this seminar in *this* hotel," and almost turned and fled.

In her current life, when she was seventeen, she had been taken prisoner in Indonesia by the Japanese in World War II. She wrote in her letter that she had "suffered physically as well as mentally from their brutality during the rest of the war. I survived, but my intestines were damaged from untreated dysentery. I was severely undernourished and I harbored a deep hatred for everything Japanese. This has continued ever since. I have sought treatment from many physicians and psychologists during the last fifty years, but I have had to live with a chronic weakness of the bowel and a deep constant pain in the solar plexus." She added that she had come to see this as the pain in the center of her being that she carried for all reviled people in the world. She continued: "Whenever I see or read about instances of brutality and inhumanity against others—especially children—the pain becomes almost unbearable."

The woman went on to tell me that after she had regressed to a past life in the seminar, she was able to see the source of her current life resentment (she didn't mention what the past life was), and that as a result of forgiving past-life circumstances, the pain that had plagued her for fifty years had completely lifted. "This old pain has disappeared and today I'm still free of it. When I left the hotel I gave a friendly greeting to the Japanese staff." She added that she had spent time talking to some of them and found them to be very pleasant, lovely people: "I feel free! Free from pain! Free from all animosity and all resentment! Truly and gloriously free and easy!"

Another seminar participant, Gerald, had a vicious relationship with his brother in his current life. As they were growing up his mother was concerned that the two brothers might kill each other because they fought so ferociously. The animosity had continued into adult life and was causing great upheaval for the entire family. In addition, Gerald felt that his hatred was taking up so much of his energy that it was holding him back from being a success in life.

Gerald regressed to a life in sixteenth-century Scandinavia, where he and his present-day brother had been rivals for the same woman. He remembered that one cold, snowy afternoon they had fought over this woman, but neither had won her hand because they had both died from their injuries. In his present life he was creating a similar scenario. When he truly forgave his rival in his past-life regression, he said he felt as though a huge weight had been lifted from his shoulders. It seemed like a miracle, he told me, because the next time he saw his brother he felt only love and compassion for him. For the first time in their lives they sat down together and truly shared from their hearts. Gerald said it was a turning point in his life, and he is now beginning to succeed in his career as well as heal lifelong hurts and resentments.

"We Don't Know the Whole Story"

To help you understand and forgive what you have done to others in past lives and what others have done to you, there is a story that I would like to share with you. I tell it often in my seminars.

A long time ago an old man lived in a Native American village. He had an extremely beautiful horse. All the people in the villages across the land had heard of this horse. It was a magnificent animal with long, shining loins. Its muscles rippled with sheen and glory every time it moved.

The Great Chief heard of this horse and sent a messenger on horseback to the old man to ask if he could purchase it. The warrior messenger raced to the old man's tepee and jumped down from his horse. Where his moccasins landed, the dust swirled in all directions. "Old man, I am here on behalf of the Great Chief. He sends his greetings and asks that he may buy your horse."

The old man had gentle dignity and quiet manners. Finally he said, "Please give my regards to the Great Chief, and please thank him for his kind offer to buy my horse. However, this horse is my friend. We are companions. I know his soul as I feel he knows mine. I cannot sell my friend."

The messenger rode away.

Two weeks later, the old man's horse disappeared.

When the villagers heard that the horse was missing, they all gathered around the old man. "Oh, old man, this is very bad fortune! You could have sold your horse to the Great Chief. Now you have no horse and no payment for the horse. What bad fortune!"

The old man looked at each villager with kind, soft eyes and said, "It is not bad fortune. It is not good fortune. We don't know the whole story. Just say the horse ran away." The villagers went away shaking their heads because they knew that this was very bad fortune.

A month later the old man's horse returned, followed by twenty other magnificent horses. Each one was spirited and bursting with vitality and exuberance. The villagers ran forward to the old man. "Oh, old man. You were right—it was not bad fortune that your horse ran away. It was good fortune. Now not only do you have your horse back but you have twenty more beautiful horses. This is good fortune!"

The old man slowly shook his head and with utmost compassion said, "It is not good. It is not bad. We don't know the whole story. Just say that the horse returned." The people went away shaking their heads. They knew that it was very, very good fortune to have so many beautiful horses.

The old man had one son, who started to break the horses. Every day the son would wake early to continue his work. One morning the old man came to watch his son. The young man had a natural grace as he swung onto the bare back of a wild pinto. The horse bucked violently to the left and twisted to the right. Suddenly with a ferocious kick of his hind legs the pinto tossed the son high in the air. The old man's son landed in a crumpled heap in the dust. Both his legs were broken.

All the inhabitants of the village gathered, with great moaning and commiserating. "Oh, no! Oh, no! Old man, you are right. Your horse returning to you was very bad fortune. Now your only son has both legs broken and is crippled. Who is going to take care of you in your old age? This is very bad fortune."

The old man pulled himself upright and with respect said, "It is not bad fortune. It is not good fortune. Just say my son broke his legs. We don't know the whole story." The villagers walked away shaking their heads. They knew it was very bad fortune for the old man.

A great war broke out across the land and the Great Chief called all the young men of the villages to battle. It was an untimely war and the villagers knew they would never see their sons again. Once more they gathered around the old man. "Old man, you are right. It is not bad fortune that your son broke his legs because, even though he is crippled, you have your son. We will never see our sons again. It was good fortune for you."

And once again the old man said, "It is not good fortune. It is not bad fortune. We don't know the whole story."

As you explore your past lives there will be times when you will experience yourself as the victim and times when you experience yourself as the victimizer. Step beyond right and wrong. Step beyond judgment. Know that who you have been and what you have experienced in the past is not good. It is not bad. You might not know the whole story.

Every experience that you have ever had—everything that has been done to you and everything that you have done to others—has been extremely important for your evolution. Even those lies that you told or those times when you were cruel or unjust have been important. Even those things that reside in shame in your soul have helped you to become who you are. All your experiences are helping you to be compassionate, whole, and loving. To the extent that you can forgive and accept yourself exactly as you are, you become a more powerful force for healing on the planet. Remember: "It is not good. It is not bad. You don't know the whole story."

Releasing Guilt

In the mid-1970s I took a trip to Italy. One morning I got up early to walk to a hill to watch the sun rise. As the first spears of light thrust over the horizon, I was overwhelmed with a deep sadness. In my mind's eye, as I looked over the valley, I was seeing not a twentieth-century scene but another time. I saw smoke rising from numerous small campfires and mixing with the morning mist. I could see that no one was up as yet. As I stood on that hill, I knew that I had been there before; I had been the Roman commander of a large army that had been fighting for a long time.

Asleep by their campfires, there were not just men but women and even some children. I felt wave after wave of grief fill me. I knew that this would be our last battle. Rather than surrender, I made the decision that we would fight our last battle on that day. I knew that I would have to speak to the troops with conviction of our victory. But I also knew that it was the day of our deaths. I knew that we would be killed without mercy. But the alternative was imprisonment, starvation, or slavery for my people. What might I have done differently? These were my people. I loved my people. Perhaps if I had been a better leader we wouldn't be facing death. These questions were superimposed on my present-day consciousness that morning.

Twenty years later, that experience in Italy was only a wisp of a memory. I was leading a reincarnation seminar in New Zealand. One of the organizers had brought her young son along to help her, and he decided to participate in one of the past-life processes. During the break he came up to me and said with soft sadness, "Denise, do you remember when we were

Romans? Do you remember when we were on a hillside looking at the smoke rise from the campfires from the night before?"

A year later, a man who had never heard of my experience on that hillside said, "Denise, do you remember when we were together in Italy as Roman soldiers? You were the commander. I fought alongside you at the last battle. It was magnificent. We all fought so gallantly. It was one of the most powerful experiences of all my lifetimes."

I was astounded! He not only remembered the same life but felt exhilarated by the experience. It was a powerful lesson for me: "I don't always know the whole story." I had felt so guilty about contributing to the deaths of so many people that I had punished myself lifetime after lifetime. I felt responsible for the experiences of others and had even presumed to know what those experiences were. I could see that I no longer needed to carry that guilt—and that in fact feeling guilty was arrogant.

All individuals create the experiences that are valuable for them and their growth. I didn't need to continue to shoulder guilt for everyone else. We *all* jointly created the experience of that last battle. This might sound like a subtle realization, but for me, it made a huge difference. Until then I had felt guilty for just about everything—even for things over which I had no control. If you told me that you had dented your car by backing into a post, most likely *I* would have felt guilty. To begin to release guilt was so freeing.

A common occurrence when one has had a disturbing dream or encountered a disturbing past life is to feel guilty about the experience. It is important to remember that there is never any cause for guilt in any dream or past-life experience that you encounter.

When you feel guilt, you are basically not taking responsibility for your actions. Guilt is a way of saying: "I really didn't do it. It really isn't my fault." It is important to acknowledge all your actions, without judgment. If you have hurt someone, make it right. If you have behaved inappropriately, alter your behavior. But do not dishonor the situation, the other person, or yourself by feeling guilty.

Guilt is always disruptive and sometimes arrogant. Forgive yourself for your past. It is important to observe and release even the thoughts and actions you may be ashamed of. Any residue of guilt that you cling to can create barriers for you.

Whenever the pain of guilt seems to attract you, remember this: If you yield to it instead of forgive yourself, you are deciding against inner peace. Therefore, say to yourself gently, but with conviction, "I accept who I am and what I have done as well as what others have done to me. I accept and forgive myself."

One valuable technique is to write down all your feelings of guilt. After you have done so, burn the pages, saying, "I release now and forever my attachments to this guilt. So be it." This may help you to begin to release guilt.

4.
HOW TO RECALL A PAST LIFE

There are numerous techniques that you can use by yourself or with a therapist to explore past lives. In this chapter I will show you specific techniques to use on your own, including preparatory exercises and full regression processes as well as how to work with a therapist or in a group. In addition, I'll describe some of the methods you can use to explore your past lives, without going into a full regression. Also, I'll present several in-depth processes for a full regression.

I strongly recommend that whenever you do any of the exercises, you carefully monitor the feelings that come up for you, and that you seek the support of a friend or therapist if you feel you need to. It can be very helpful to talk out whatever comes up for you, whether it is painful or joyous. Sharing this work with someone who is close to you in this life is a wonderful and important way to integrate material from past lives into your present experience. Be sure to choose this companion carefully—make sure it is someone who truly cherishes you and will not make light of your efforts.

Just Making It Up

People in my seminars sometimes say, "But I'm just making this up!" when they get in touch with a past life during a process. Of course you are making it up. Where do you think all of life came from? You are always "making it up," no matter what you are experiencing. Just let go. Allow your imagination free rein, without constantly questioning the images, and you will begin to receive more and more accurate information regarding your past. When you first try to discover your past lives, the images are often jumbled—just like trying to remember events from your childhood. But the more you practice, the clearer the images become. As you accumulate past-life clues, be willing to use your imagination, as this will often allow a more accurate picture to unfold.

Past-Life Clues

> *Through analysis of your present strong tendencies you can pretty accurately surmise what kind of life you led before.*
>
> —Paramahansa Yogananda, *Man's Eternal Quest*

You might find it valuable to explore your current life for clues to your past lives. I strongly recommend that you do the following exercise before advancing to the past-life regression process at the end of this chapter. This exercise is a very powerful way to begin to open the door for spontaneous past-life recall in your dreams or regressions, without requiring you to go into an altered state of consciousness. You might think of yourself as a "past-life detective" as you amass clues from your affinities and experiences in your current life.

No single clue can give you all the answers, but if you put the clues together you can begin to piece together the puzzle of who you might have been. To begin the exercise, write each of the following topics on top of a separate sheet of paper and then list your experiences and affinities beneath each topic.

- Childhood games
- Clothing styles
- Architecture
- Food preferences
- Geographical locations
- Climates
- Cultures
- Time periods or historical events
- Déjà vu experiences
- Occupations
- Talents and abilities
- Race and heritage
- Books and films
- Animals and pets
- Personality traits and mannerisms
- Fears and phobias
- Injuries, diseases, and scars
- Dreams

For example, on the top of one sheet write: Food Preferences. Then list your favorite kinds of food, such as French and Chinese. On each sheet write down all the clues that you can gather for that topic. Place the completed sheets side by side so that a larger picture can begin to form. When I did this exercise, I saw that I had many clues to indicate a past life in Japan. I've always loved the simple lines of traditional Japanese architecture. In my current life, not only did I live for more than two years in a Japanese Buddhist monastery, but I studied Japanese culture for two years in college. I also studied the Japanese tea ceremony and ikebana (Japanese flower arranging), and I have trained in the Japanese healing systems of Reiki and Shiatsu. My favorite restaurants are Japanese. In addition, there was a period in my life when I saw every samurai movie I could. To me, Toshiro Mifune is a bigger star than Robert Redford. Looking at these clues as a "reincarnation detective," it makes sense that I had a past life in the Far East.

As you make your lists, notice your emotional response regarding each topic. For example, under the animals-and-pets category, notice if there is any particular animal with which you have a close affinity or of which you have always been afraid. I know a man who has a very close affinity with horses who was a Mongolian in a past life. In that life he loved his horse even more than his wife. In the category of personality traits and mannerisms, note any personal mannerisms that you have. I know a woman who rubs her throat whenever she is under stress. In a past life she was stabbed in the throat.

Patterns should begin to emerge as you gather your clues. How will you know if you are accurate? How can you learn to distinguish between simple fascination and a stirring of deep, inner knowing? Usually a good indication is your emotional response: It just feels right; you have a gut reaction. If you are unsure, be still for a while and meditate on the ideas that are beginning to form from your clues. Even if you are not completely clear, sooner or later your subconscious will begin to show you the way to greater understanding. In particular, watch your dreams after you have done this exercise. They should become more vivid with past-life images.

CHILDHOOD GAMES

Most common childhood games are the result of programming by society. A little girl might be given a baby doll and told that she is the mother. Her childhood games of playing mother to her babies are, in part, conditioned by her culture. Other childhood games are the result of a child symbolically imitating or acting out the behavior of adults. A little boy might observe his father doing repairs around the house. He will then fashion a makeshift hammer and play at making bookshelves. Sometimes, however, childhood games are a residue of memories from past lives. As you examine the games that you spontaneously played as a child, look for possible reflections of what could be one of your past lives.

I have a friend who, as a child, used to make a prisonlike structure out of cardboard. She would then get inside it and pretend that she was starving. She got her childhood friends to "sneak" small pieces of dried bread to her. She said that later, when she was an adult, she spontaneously remembered living in a German concentration camp. As soon as she recalled that past life, she understood why she had played that game over and over again as a child. She was reenacting a very significant time in a past life.

When I was six I used to go alone into the woods by our house. I spent hours picking small bits of different plants and tasting them. I would bring a bunch of my selected plants home, let them dry, and then try to grind them up into a powder. I called my mixtures "medicine." I would try to get my friends to take some of my "medicine" if they weren't feeling well. I believe that this game was based on my memories as a Blackfoot Indian gathering herbs for medicine for her tribal people. A skeptic might say that my childhood game could have been a result of programming by stories that I had heard or by information that I had subconsciously absorbed. But if that was the case, why did I fixate on one particular piece of information to the exclusion of all others? And how does a skeptic explain a child who is a master musician even though his parents are not musically talented? Though it is impossible to prove beyond a doubt the fact of reincarnation, it is enormously valuable to observe childhood games, for they often hold important keys to understanding past lives.

The younger the child, usually the more potent the past-life memories. My grandmother told me that when I was three, I used to get very irritated with her because she didn't remember our life together as sisters. She said I would plaintively ask again and again, "Don't you remember?" When Meadow, my daughter, was three, she used to talk about her servants. I found that very curious, considering that we lived in a very casual way and often ate our meals sitting on the floor. (This can probably be traced to my Native American life, when I sat on the ground by the fire to eat.) However, even as a three-year-old, Meadow insisted on sitting at the table, placing numerous spoons, forks, and knives very neatly next to her plate as if in a formal table setting. She also used to ask me to lay her clothes out on the bed "because my servants used to lay out my clothes for me."

When her friends came to play, Meadow would organize very genteel games with elaborate tea parties. One day her friends went outside to play and I encouraged her to go with them. She responded gravely, "I'm not allowed to play with other children. I'm not allowed to get my clothes soiled." The pain and sadness of a lonely royal or formal past life filtered through into her childhood games. Childhood attitudes can often be attributed to environment or upbringing, but not in her case, for my husband and I are down-home kind of people. Meadow continues to be quite the lady. However, I can't help but think that she chose us as parents to balance a past life that was extremely formal and rigid.

CLOTHING STYLES

Often, a valuable clue to your past lives can be found in the fashion styles to which you are drawn. For example, if you prefer long, flowing scarves and soft loose fabrics, and you love the tall, stately stone pillars of Greek architecture, you might have had a previous life in ancient Greece. Of course, there could be many reasons why you choose those particular clothes, but as you begin to assemble clues, your style preference can be very helpful in understanding the whole picture.

Are you attracted to a gypsy style, peasant style, military style, or any particular ethnic style? Do you enjoy wearing long dresses or dinner jackets, or do you loathe formal wear and just like to feel comfortable? Are there any particular styles of hats that you have worn? I knew an American man who always wore a Greek cap; he discovered that he had been a Greek sailor. A Frenchman I knew continually wore a cowboy hat; he discovered that he had lived as a cowboy in the nineteenth-century Wild West. An Australian woman who always wore a beret found that she had been in the French Resistance during World War II. The colors of your clothing may also have past-life significance. I knew a woman who always wore saffron yellow—it was more or less her trademark. Regressed to a past life, she recalled being a Hindu monk in India, wearing saffron-colored robes every day.

ARCHITECTURE

Examine the architecture styles to which you are attracted. Are you fascinated by Tudor, Georgian, or Victorian architecture, or are you interested in structures such as cabins, tepees, yurts, and cliff dwellings, or perhaps castles or Greek temples? What kind of architecture do you like? What kind do you dislike?

FOOD PREFERENCES

If asked to pick the type of food that you most enjoy, would you go for Indian, Chinese, Thai, Japanese, French, Italian, Greek, African, Spanish, Mexican, English, Scandinavian, German, Russian, Vietnamese, Hungarian, or some other type of food? Is there a particular food or type of food that you prefer? For example, if you really love pineapples and papayas, this might indicate that you lived in a tropical climate. If you are passionate about pickled herring, this might indicate a life in Scandinavia. Is there a food to which you are allergic? Food allergies can, of course, come from many sources, but I have had clients who discovered that their food allergies had their origins in a past life.

GEOGRAPHICAL LOCATIONS

Are there countries to which you are attracted or that you have always wanted to visit? Perhaps there is a country that you have visited many times. Is there a country toward which you feel a repulsion and never want to visit? One seminar participant discovered that his lifelong repulsion to traveling to India had its source in an unhappy lifetime in one of that country's northern regions. Do you feel an affinity to a particular kind of landscape, such as mountains, deserts, hills, misty moors, meadowlands, or the sea? What is your favorite kind of environment? Write down geographical locations that evoke an emotional response, whether positive or negative.

CLIMATES

In what climate do you feel emotionally most comfortable? Do you like extreme, arid heat? If so, perhaps you lived in a desert. Do you like moist, tropical climates, or do you prefer the clean, crisp coolness of winter snow? Imagine yourself in different climates and note your different emotional responses to each.

CULTURES

Do certain cultures interest you? Are you fascinated by the American Indian culture, for instance, or by the ancient Egyptian culture or by the Aztecs'? Are there designs or symbols that appeal to you? Look at those of Celtic, Egyptian, Maori, Native American, African, Chinese, Japanese, Indian, Viking, Roman, and Middle Eastern cultures. Do any of them feel familiar to you?

TIME PERIODS OR HISTORICAL EVENTS

Examine periods in time that have interested you in your present life. Cast your mind back to your school days. Was there a particular period such as the Stone Age, the Bronze Age, the time of the pharaohs, the Middle Ages, the Renaissance, or the Industrial Revolution that appealed to you then? Are there historical events that greatly interest you now such as the Armada, the French Revolution, or World War I? Consult any brief world-history reference work to see if there are periods that stand out in your mind. Remember, however, that many books of this kind ignore native cultures, so you will have to look in anthropology books for this type of information.

DÉJÀ VU EXPERIENCES

If you have ever been in a particular place for the first time and felt that you had been there before, write that down. Also note occasions when you have met someone and felt that you knew him or her already. Psychologists say that déjà vu experiences occur when the scene that you are observing becomes available to your conscious mind a split second before you are consciously aware of it. You feel that you have seen the scene before because indeed you have—a split second earlier. However, I have found a direct correlation between déjà vu experiences and past lives. These experiences are very important in your past-life exploration. Carefully record all your déjà vu experiences.

I once had a very powerful déjà vu experience that gave me an understanding of one of my past lives. More than twenty years ago, I was sightseeing in Venice and a girlfriend and I decided to hire a gondola to visit some of the neighboring islands. One particular island seemed to glisten more brightly than the others in the distant haze, and I pointed it out to our gondolier. This beguiling gem in the sea seemed to be beckoning to me. Soon we landed at a small jetty.

As I disembarked, a balding, plump Franciscan monk came scurrying out to greet us. He spoke some English and offered to give me a tour of the island, which was entirely taken up by his monastery and its grounds. As I followed him, I was swept away by an overwhelming feeling of déjà vu. I felt so comfortable on that island—I knew exactly what lay around each corner even before we reached it. Images and forgotten memories flooded my consciousness. How could it be that I knew my way so clearly? I had never heard of this island before. Suddenly, as we rounded a corner, I viewed a scene far different from the one I was remembering. Quite spontaneously, I exclaimed, "Oh, this is new!" With an astonished look the monk replied, "It is new to the original structure . . . but it is more than six hundred years old." To my amazement, I had unearthed memories of being a monk on that lovely island more than six hundred years before.

OCCUPATIONS

Often the occupations to which we are drawn are the same as our past-life occupations or have similar features. This seems especially true of occupations in early life. For example, one man whom I regressed had been a piano maker in Germany in a past life. In this life, when he was growing up he learned to play the piano and in his twenties he became a carpenter. Both occupations are connected with his life as a piano maker. He is now neither a pianist nor a carpenter but an artist. I believe that he has completed the karma from that German life, so he is no longer involved in occupations similar to those he had in that past life.

TALENTS AND ABILITIES

Many of the abilities that come to you spontaneously and easily can be attributed to past lives. Perhaps child prodigies such as Mozart, who played the harpsichord with great virtuosity at an early age, gained their abilities from a past life. Examining your spontaneous and natural abilities might give additional clues to who you were.

One Saturday morning our daughter announced that she wanted to go skating. She had been watching a skating competition on television the evening before and had been enthralled by its beauty and grace. My husband is usually very slow to get going in the morning, so I was astounded when he immediately agreed—especially since he had never ice skated in his life.

Our experiences when we got to the rink surprised me greatly. My daughter had roller skated before but never ice skated. Very quickly her ankles began to wobble and she plopped down on the ice. I had skated a lot as a child but I was rusty and shaky. As I helped Meadow up from the ice, we looked for David, the nonskater. Just at that moment he sailed past with smooth, graceful, gliding movements. He turned in circles. He skated backward. He skated fast. He skated slowly. He completed wondrous spins and turns. Astonishing! Then, after several minutes of pirouetting around the rink, his feet suddenly flew out from under him and he pulled a muscle in his knee. It was as though something inside him knew exactly how to skate, but his muscles weren't prepared to move in those directions. Previously he had recalled a life as a city official in Holland, where he had often skated on canals and frozen ponds. I believe that his memories of ice skating in Holland had filtered through from his past.

RACE AND HERITAGE

There is often a correlation between a person's cultural and/or racial heritage and the types of past lives they have had. This correlation is not always in evidence, and to date there has been very little research into this phenomenon. However, people will often have an ancestor in a culture in which they have had a past life. A man whose great-grandfather came from Spain might discover that he himself was Spanish in a previous lifetime.

BOOKS AND FILMS

Finding clues to your past lives can be as easy as looking through travel books or *National Geographic* magazine to observe your reactions to various scenes. Read about different cultures in an encyclopedia and note which ones you find interesting. Look at pictures of different environments and notice how they affect you. For example, look at some photographs of desert scenes and see if you have any emotional reactions to them. If you do feel a response, use your imagination to put yourself in the photograph. Imagine what you might have looked like or what kind of life might have fit in with the photograph.

Note the kinds of books to which you have been attracted during your life. As a child I read every book that I could find about the Amazon. I was fascinated by those steamy jungle scenes and completely entranced by the abundance of wildlife, especially the anacondas. I also loved going to the zoo to look at the large snakes and even got my parents to introduce me to a snake expert. Holding an anaconda and a boa constrictor was one of the greatest thrills of my childhood. I even raised and bred snakes. But there was nothing in my upbringing to suggest an interest in snakes or the jungle.

Examining the types of books and films that attract you is very valuable in your exploration of past lives. Make a list of the images and scenes in your favorite books and movies that have particularly impressed you.

ANIMALS AND PETS

Do you feel especially drawn to certain kinds of animals? When you are with these animals, do you feel able to communicate with them? This type of experience may be related to a past life in which you had extensive contact with a particular kind of animal. Perhaps you were a horse trainer or a farmer. Or perhaps, at some point in time, your only friend was an animal. The emotional solace provided by that relationship may have been the one thing that kept you going through an incredibly difficult experience. There are accounts of prisoners who formed relationships with rats in their cells, saving a portion of their meager rations to feed their animal friends. These acts of unselfishness, along with the gratitude of the animals, helped them to stay sane.

To the ancient Egyptians, cats were gods. Relics of that time are filled with regal pictures of cats acting out the civilization's most important myths. In fact, cats were so honored that many of them were embalmed along with their owners when they died. If you have had a lifelong affinity with cats, nearly to the point of worshiping them, you might have had a life in ancient Egypt.

PERSONALITY TRAITS AND MANNERISMS

More clues to your past lives can be found through studying the mannerisms and personality traits that make you unique. Of course, many of these characteristics can be traced to events and influences in your present life. However, people often exhibit types of behavior that seem, on the surface, to make no sense in terms of their personal history. For example, a man who is normally very mild-mannered, and who comes from a refined and educated family who were kind and never lost their tempers, might find that whenever he witnesses cruelty to children he feels sudden, violent anger and has to restrain himself from responding. He may even want to kill someone for shouting at their children. In a past life this man may have been in an orphanage where children were never respected and often were treated cruelly.

Personal mannerisms that are completely out of keeping with one's upbringing can also be explained through exploration of past lives. Sometimes, people who grew up in poverty and later became extremely wealthy will report that they have always loved luxurious things and that they lived as though they had them even under the worst of conditions. They had refined mannerisms and behaved as though they were royalty. It is likely that such people experienced privilege in previous lifetimes, and therefore knew instinctively how to act and how to re-create these conditions in this lifetime.

FEARS AND PHOBIAS

Many people cannot explain their fears and phobias even after years of traditional therapy. Sometimes these problems can be unraveled only by working through traumas experienced during past lives. For example, a woman might have such an extreme fear of snakes that it inhibits her ability to do things she would otherwise enjoy. She might be afraid to walk in the woods for fear of seeing a snake. Nightmares about snakes may have kept her awake for weeks at a time. Finally, through past-life regression, such an individual may discover that she was once lowered into a snake pit as punishment for a petty crime in an ancient and barbarous culture in which she once lived. The subconscious fear that this could happen to her for some small thing that she might unwittingly do in this life can haunt her for years, until she becomes aware of the original source of her fear.

Examination of our most persistent fears and phobias that seem unrelated to the facts of our present existence can be a very useful tool for deciphering clues to our past lives. Many people choose to do past-life work because fearful experiences in past lives are often re-created in the present. Thus, you will find that whatever you fear will return again and again to your life until you overcome it. This is a cosmic law. So, examine your fears and phobias. You might even imagine possible scenarios to accompany them in order to gain further insight into who you were.

INJURIES, DISEASES, AND SCARS

In my past-life regressions I have found a definite correlation between the injuries, diseases, and even scars that we have in this life and what has occurred in other lives. In regression, a woman vividly remembered having been shot in the forehead. Interestingly, this woman found an unusual, small indentation beneath her hairline that looked as if a small bullet had penetrated there. Another individual had developed a dreadful, blistering rash as a thirteen-year-old. As an adult, during a regression she experienced burning to death as a thirteen-year-old servant in a past life in Spain. When she reached the same age in her present life, her subconscious activated that memory. This subconscious association contributed to the development of a rash that resembled burns. I have found that we often develop physical conditions at an age close to that at which we experienced the onset of the condition in a past life. Even birthmarks can carry clues to past lives. I suggest you look at your birthmarks or scars and ask yourself what might have made those marks, then notice any images or feelings that well up from within you.

DREAMS

One of the most powerful ways to gain understanding of past lives without undergoing a regression is through observing your dreams (see chapter 5 for more information). Every dream gives you secret messages regarding not only your current life and relationships but those in the past and even the future.

Once you have compiled all your lists of clues, study this information and start to form a picture of what some of your past-life scenarios might be. This information can be useful for further past-life work and can also provide you with a feeling of security—you can gain some sense of where you will be traveling, without having to feel as if you are just leaping into the dark. In the following sections I will discuss methods for regression that will take you directly into the past you have been exploring in a tentative way, so that you can acquire a more focused view of your past lives.

Regression

The most common method of past-life regression involves using your powers of visualization. Visualization is an excellent technique because it allows you to reach the subconscious—and once reached, your subconscious mind cannot tell the difference between a real experience and one that is vividly imagined. It is medically and scientifically recognized that visualized images actually bring about psychological and even physiological changes, in some cases to almost the same degree as direct experience.

A study at the University of Chicago demonstrated the power of visualization. College students were divided into three groups and their basketball shooting abilities were noted. The different groups were observed performing foul shots, each group having undergone a different kind of mental preparation. (Foul shots are when a player stands on a certain line and throws the ball to the hoop. The distance between the hoop and the player is always the same, and the action of the game is halted while the player attempts the shot.) Group 1 did not practice foul shots for the thirty days of the experiment, and at the end of that time showed no improvement. Group 2 practiced foul shots every day for thirty days and showed a

24 percent improvement. Group 3 practiced foul shots only in their minds for thirty days, and showed an astonishing 23 percent improvement.

The significance of this phenomenon can be applied to past-life therapy. If you visualize a journey to a past life and resolve it, your subconscious will recognize that inner journey as a real journey—and recognize the resolution that you have come to as a real one.

To ensure that your regression is a positive experience, pick an emotionally and physically safe place in your home in which to do it. Select a time when you are not overwhelmed by external stresses. Finally, make sure that someone whom you care about and trust is ready to help you process whatever comes up for you, if you feel you might need such assistance. This can be helpful not only for dealing with negative emotions but for sorting out the positive ones. A good discussion with a friend can be extremely valuable for getting a clear perspective on things and piecing together a whole picture from fragments of information.

It is important that you thoroughly familiarize yourself with the resolution techniques described in chapter 6 before you try out any of the full regression processes. You need to learn ways to resolve the experiences you may encounter in your past life in order to avoid retraumatizing yourself. You don't want just to relive your previous scenarios—you want to resolve them.

When doing past-life processes, you will become aware only of lifetimes that reflect something with which you are dealing in your present life. Whatever lifetime you see will contain people, situations, or issues that symbolize those in your present life. The more you practice these exercises, and the more past-life experiences you become aware of and resolve, the more balanced you will be in your current life.

Visualization Technique

Step 1. Enter a Sanctuary

To begin your visual journey to the past I usually suggest that you first become very relaxed (see page 100). Then imagine going to a place in nature; this can be either a place that you have actually been where you felt at peace, or an imaginary place. If you have difficulty visualizing, as some people do, I suggest that you get a *sense* of being in nature using other senses besides sight. To do this you might imagine the sounds around you—the singing of birds, the sound of a faraway waterfall, the babble of a trickling brook. Try to get a sense of the smells and physical sensations you might experience in nature. For example, imagine yourself out in the woods. Do you smell the dampness of spongy moss under your feet? Does the piercing smell of fresh air and pine trees clear out your head? Can you feel the warmth of the sun penetrate your body as you walk along, or perhaps as you lie stretched out on a smooth, sun-baked rock?

Visualizing yourself in nature will help create a feeling of peace and safety before going on to your past-life regression. You will feel the connection with the earth, and this provides a sense of great comfort for many people. I usually have my clients meet their guides at this time (see chapter 7). This increases the feeling of safety and well-being before stepping into the past.

Step 2. Transition Options

Once you have imagined a place in nature, it is important to have a transition before stepping into a past life. You will be traveling a long way in terms of time, and sometimes in terms of distance. You can think of these transition exercises as a kind of gentle vehicle that will carry you where you want to go, so that you arrive safe and sound and with a minimum of culture shock. It is important to recognize that you need such a mechanism in order to let your mind and body adjust to the suspension of linear time and space.

A transition is also helpful because regression exercises can cause very intense emotions, ranging from exhilaration and joy to terror or intense grief, to surge to the surface.

Here are several methods that can help you to make a successful transition, which is the first stage to the regression exercises.

TIME TUNNEL

Leave your imagined safe place, or nature sanctuary, and walk into a time tunnel. You might count the steps or imagine getting closer and closer until you finally step into a past life.

BRIDGE OF TIME

While you are in nature, a bridge appears. You climb up the bridge high above the clouds. As you continue your journey, you descend down the bridge through the clouds into a past life.

RIVER OF TIME

You step into a small boat lined with soft pillows. You recline on the pillows and watch the clouds overhead while the boat travels of its own volition down the river of time, taking you to a past life.

ELEVATOR

Get into the cosmic elevator. Every floor number on the lighted panel represents a different life. You can either push a button or wait for the elevator to stop. When the doors open, you step into a past life.

ROOM OF DOORS

You enter a circular room with many doors, or walk down a hallway lined with doors on either side. Each door opens to one of your past lives. If you like, imagine small windows to look through in each door before you open it.

TIME MACHINE

A time machine appears in your sanctuary. You step in and the machine lifts up into the clouds. When it descends, you are in a past life. You can even have a panel in the time machine that shows you the exact date on which you have arrived.

MISTS OF TIME

Your sanctuary in nature becomes very misty. As you walk into the mists you know that an amazing transition is occurring—your body is going through a metamorphosis. Although you cannot see it happening, you can feel your body change as it becomes the body you occupied in a past life. Then you step into your past life.

There are many variations on the methods described above. Try them out to see which ones work best for you.

Step 3. Journey into a Past Life

After your transition from your sanctuary in nature, the next step is actually to visualize a past life. The meditation below gives an example of how to do this.

★ ★ ★

To program yourself for past-life recall, ask someone to read the following to you in a very soothing voice. You can also tape-record yourself reading the process and play it back. (If you are making a tape, substitute "I" for "you.")

Start by getting your body into a very relaxed position, either sitting or reclining. Now take some very deep, relaxed breaths. With each breath you take, you are becoming more and more relaxed. Each breath you take, each sound you hear, allows you to become more and more relaxed.

Now put your attention on your left foot and feel it relax. It is now completely relaxed. Now put your awareness in your right foot and feel it completely let go and relax. Allow that delicious feeling of relaxation to roll up your left leg and just let it relax. Good. Now put your awareness in your right leg and let that same wonderful feeling of relaxation roll up it. Now let your right leg completely relax. Continue to feel a slow wave of relaxation roll up from your feet, through your legs, up your torso, out through your arms and hands and up and out of the top of your head. Your entire body is now relaxed and warm and comfortable. Take one very deep breath and totally relax and let go.

Now imagine you are walking across a field. It's a warm day and you are filled with the full, rich scent of the grass. You hear the gentle drone of insects and the summer songs of birds . . . these sounds fill the air with a soothing, rhythmic cadence. A mist begins to rise from the fields and a stillness fills the air. In the distance you hear the gentle sounds of a river lapping against the bank. You approach the river. The mists are becoming very thick. As you reach the edge of the river, you notice a sturdy bridge crossing it. The mist has become so thick that you can't see the other side of the bridge. In fact, you can see only a few feet in front of you as you step onto it. With each step you take, you know you are nearing one of your past lives. You are crossing the ever-flowing river of time. I shall count from 1 to 22. When I reach 22, you will step off the bridge at a time far back, before you came into your present body. Now, 1—2—3—4 . . . with each step you take, the swirling, mystical mist seems to embrace you with warmth and love . . . 5—6—7—8—9 . . . you are aware of a very loving presence guiding and protecting your every step; 10—11—12—13—14—15—16—17 . . . the fog is beginning to thin; 18—19 . . . the end of the bridge is near; 20—21—22. . . . Step off the bridge.

You have arrived in another time, in one of your past lives. The mist has completely cleared. Look down at your feet. Are they the feet of a man or a woman? Are they young feet or old feet? Are you standing outside or inside? What surface are you standing on? Sand? Stone? Tile? A wooden floor? Grass? What covering do you have on your feet? What clothes do you have on? Look around and note what you perceive. Are you in the country or the city? If there are any buildings, notice the architecture. Are there any people nearby? If there are, listen to them speaking. What language does it sound like? Are there any people who resemble people in your present life? As you explore and perceive this life, notice your feelings and emotions. How does it feel to be in this life? You have a few minutes to explore this life. . . . You may do it now.

Now go to a time in this lifetime that was very significant or important to you. You have a short while to experience what is happening and to determine how you feel about these circumstances.

Now go forward in time in the past life that you are exploring . . . go forward to the time when you are about to shed your body and pass over to the spirit world. How did you die? Was it slowly or suddenly? What people were around you? Were you reluctant or glad to go? In spiritual retrospect, the process of dying is seldom recognized as a painful event, and there is usually a great sigh of relief once you realize you have passed over. It's like returning home after a long absence. You have a minute to observe this significant event in your past life. You may do this now.

Now go forward into the spirit world. From your perspective in the spirit world, what did you learn from that past life? Were there any fears or concerns from that life that are present in your life today?

As you realize where those fears originated, you know that they are not real, and it is simple to release them. Just release them. You know that you can create your life in the present to be exactly the way you want it. You know that you can choose freely without programming from other lives.

Now it is time to let that previous life fade away and return to your present life. Just let the past life fade away . . . just drift away.

As you move more and more toward normal waking awareness, you feel good, strong, and empowered. You have stepped into your far past with courage and have looked without judgment at who and what you were. By this very looking, your present life is enhanced and enriched. By this very observing, you have taken a step closer to the divinity within you. You are free to explore any past life, and the knowledge you gain creates the space for your life to be more fulfilling and whole.

I'm going to count from 1 to 5. When I reach 5, you will be totally awake and aware. Now, 1—2 . . . your body is healthy and strong; 3 . . . more and more awake; 4 . . . your eyes feel as if they have been bathed in fresh, cool spring water; 5 . . . wide awake and feeling great. Open your eyes now. Stretch and enjoy the beauty of the day.

"Follow the Feeling" Technique

Begin this technique by deciding the area of your life with which you would like assistance. These are some areas that you might consider:

- Forgiveness for others
- Forgiveness for yourself
- Health issues
- Fears or phobias
- Talents or strengths you want to reawaken
- Blockages in your life

Step 1. Locate the Body Sensation

Identify the issue in your life that you want to work with. Then just relax. Allow yourself to be aware of what emotion or feeling you might associate with your area of concern. Then feel that emotion. To feel emotions, locate where they are causing changes in your body. For example, you might locate fear as a tightening feeling in the center of your chest, or you could be holding your breath. Now go through your body and locate the area where you feel the emotion associated with the issue on which you want to work.

For example, maybe you have been angry with your father for mistreating you during childhood, but now you want to forgive him. Think about your father and the mistreatment you suffered. Feel the anger. Now, use your imagination to travel inside your body and find the spot where you feel the anger. If the anger feels like a lump in your chest, focus your entire attention there and ask yourself what this feeling might look like. Use the following criteria:

- color
- size
- shape
- texture

To understand how to do this, imagine that you can "see" feelings inside your body. What color might they be? Repeat the process for size, shape, and texture. For example, your anger at your father might "look" oblong and dark blue, about the size of a football, residing in the center of your chest. Answering these questions helps to activate the stored memories in your body by focusing attention on them. This is a powerful technique, because past-life memories are lodged not just in your brain but in your body. Using the body is an excellent way to access past lives.

Step 2. Regress

Keeping your awareness on the particular place in your body that you have chosen, notice any spontaneous memories that surface. If the memories are from last week rather than a past life, that's all right. Ask to see an earlier, similar memory. Keep regressing through earlier memories until you reach one that seems the likely source of your difficulty. At that point, you can use any of the resolution techniques described in chapter 6.

Regression Technique

This simple technique allows you to become very relaxed and begin to go backward in time.

Step 1. Recall

- yesterday
- last week
- last month
- last year
- childhood

- in womb
- past life

Step 2. Resolution (see Chapter 6)

Other Techniques

LOOK IN A MIRROR

Become very still and relaxed. In a dimly lit room—light a candle—stare at your reflection in a mirror. Sometimes your face will change shape and you can begin to see how you might have looked in a past life. Periodically close your eyes and see if any images arise spontaneously. Relax. Open your mind to the infinity of the universe and the endless possibilities in your own past. If you begin to feel unsure or disoriented, take a break and try again later. Or you might want to try a variation of this technique, as described below.

ONE-ON-ONE

This is similar to the mirror technique except that you do it with a friend. It is important to choose someone whom you trust deeply and who can help you process whatever feelings come up.

Working with someone else can be done in one of two ways. You can each look into the other's face and mutually search for clues as to who the other person was in another life. Or one person can look at the other as he or she simply sits still and relaxes. In either case, you will be concentrating on the face of your partner in the same way as you looked at your face in the mirror exercise. Often you will start to see the other's face change and he will seem to look different. Sometimes he may look to be of the opposite gender, or of a different race or age. Trust your intuition as you gain clues to who the person may have been.

GROUP REGRESSION

Most of my work now is with groups, usually two hundred at a time. I find this very effective because there is a tremendous amount of energy available in a large group. If you choose to be regressed in a large group, it is important that the person leading the regression has many years of experience and is someone about whom you feel good. I recommend that you get personal references from people who have attended the group regression you are considering. Attending a group recession can be exhilarating because of the remarkable synchronicity and coincidences that often occur.

TAPES

Some people use regression tapes quite successfully. The first time I recorded my regression tapes, the engineer in the recording booth—who did not believe in past lives—fell off his stool and spontaneously got in touch with a past life. (See page 179 for information on obtaining my past-life regression tapes.)

PAST-LIFE THERAPIST

Some issues in life require the help of a therapist. One indication that you might need the assistance of a therapist is if the feelings you are experiencing are interfering with your ability to go about your normal life. If you feel completely overwhelmed and cannot cope, get help. The first step is to seek references from people you trust. It's also a good idea to check the certification and credentials of the therapist you choose.

Understand that while some painful things may come up, you should never feel worse overall than you did before you started therapy. Working with the person you choose should bring you a sense of relief, and you must believe that he or she respects you and is deserving of your deepest trust.

DREAMS

One of the most powerful ways to connect with past lives is through your dreams, so I have devoted chapter 5 to that subject.

The foregoing are just a few of the many techniques that can be used to access past lives. In your past-life processes, remember that different chronological times in your life will reflect different past lives you have had.

As your current life at this moment mirrors one particular past life, you will usually be surrounded or closely involved with people from that life. For example, Sarah was very absorbed with her spiritual path and became involved with her local church. She began to assist at the church's Sunday morning children's group and developed a number of new friendships within the congregation. At the same time, she developed a fascination with candles and incense. In a past-life regression she discovered that she had been a nun in the south of France—where they had burned many candles and used incense—and found that her new church friends had all been nuns at the same abbey. In their shared past life they had all cared for orphaned children. They were all drawn together again in similar circumstances to complete any karma they may have accrued together in their past life.

Remember to have fun in your past-life explorations. Enjoy the process and let go of concerns about being always historically correct—this makes it easier for your subconscious mind to bring up past-life memories. If you are constantly questioning the validity of the historical facts of your past life, you can lose the psychological value of your exploration and it becomes more difficult to recall your past life accurately. It would be as if you were trying to remember your present-life twelfth birthday party. If your conscious mind kept saying, "No, that can't be right," it would become increasingly difficult to remember your birthday.

Through the use of past-life recall exercises, you can open the door to the past and can begin to release limitations from past lives and have a more beautiful, loving future. Past-life exploration, through wakeful exploration and through your dreams, can help you gain an unparalleled understanding of your present-life circumstances.

5. DREAMS AND PAST LIVES

The question of karma is obscure to me, as is also the problem of personal rebirth . . . Recently, however, I observed in myself a series of dreams which would seem to describe the process of reincarnation.

—C. G. Jung, *Memories, Dreams, Reflections*

It is commonly accepted that dreams can give you potent information about your present. These mysterious messages from your mind can warn you of danger, or they may contain the seeds for creative inspiration. Einstein stated that his theory of relativity came as a result of a dream; in fact, many of his discoveries came as a result of dreams.

In addition, these nocturnal visions can serve as a gateway to the mystic arenas of the night for inner-dimensional travel and communication with the inner realms. They can be a springboard for night healing, astral travel, and soul searching. Dreams can foretell the future and give you valuable information about the past. They are a viable way for your guides to communicate directly with you without going through the censor of your conscious mind. Importantly, dreams can also be a door for you to pass through to travel through time and space in order to step into a past life.

D. Scott Rogo of John F. Kennedy University in California did some very interesting research regarding reincarnation memories in dreams. He placed advertisements in metaphysical-oriented magazines to elicit responses from anyone who had experienced past-life memories other than through regression. In his book *The Search for Yesterday*, Rogo reported that the largest group of credible recollections of past lives came from dreams.

When you are dreaming, your mind is much less likely to be confined by the limits of logic, which is why it is often the easiest way to connect with your past lives. Even people who don't believe in reincarnation have reported dreams in which they participated in activities at another time in history. This can, of course, be attributed to a recently seen movie or a recently read book. However, there are some qualities that distinguish past-life dreams from ordinary ones.

Past-life dreams seem much more real than conventional dreams: the colors are brighter, edges and corners are sharper, and everything seems much more vivid and clear. Frederick Lenz, a psychologist with the New School for Social Research, reports in his book *Lifetimes* that many subjects were aware and very strongly affected when their dreams were of former lives. When past-life dreams recur, as they often do, usually there is some unresolved issue that is trying desperately to filter through to consciousness. These dreams can be interpreted as an invitation for us to resolve that past-life conflict or difficulty.

Dreams, Past Lives, and the New Harmonics

I believe that in the next few years there will be a huge increase in the number of past-life images appearing in dreams. Our dreams are increasingly going to act as filtering grounds for past-life issues that are influencing our present and struggling to reach resolution.

Here is a metaphor I use to explain why our dreams are so important for resolving past-life issues. Imagine the midnight darkness of a desert. The sky is punctuated by exquisite shimmering stars. A celestial canopy radiates above, as cars below wind their way along a desert road. Most of the occupants are enjoying the grand beauty of the night. However, a few cars have their radios turned on, but since they are miles away from any radio stations they can't pick up anything. Then, from the farthest reaches of the universe, CRS (Cosmic Radio Station) begins to broadcast toward the earth.

Those with their radios on begin to hear static, as waves of increasingly higher frequency are projected to our planet. As the intensity increases, the static also increases, until fine-tuning brings the signals in clearly. Then, all mental and physical tensions ease completely. And all who are listening hear the most exquisite music—music so soothing and beautiful that cares and concerns begin to fade away. The irritations and difficulties of life begin to dissolve and there is a feeling of infinite peace. The very special music from CRS stirs in the depths of the soul a remembrance of a far and distant place . . . a place filled with an abundance of light, compassion, and fulfillment.

Right now, new frequencies and energies are flooding our planet. For many, dreamtime is becoming like a turned-on radio. Because of the nonsequential, intuitive nature of your dreams, you will first "hear" many of those "CRS" frequencies through the symbols and images in your dreams. Dreams are an untapped source of enormous potential for the planetary release that is occurring. In the months and years ahead, many past-life images and symbols will flood your dreams. These new harmonics will stimulate old blockages that have resided deep within you for lifetimes. Your dreams and your life may feel as if they are filled with static. As these blockages release, you will begin to remember who you truly are, and the static will begin to ease, metamorphosing into a beauty you have not known before.

As a child I had a recurring nightmare: There was a furnace with an open door. I could see the flames and feel the intense heat. Bodies of adults and children were being put into the furnace. Every morning, I would wake up feeling an abhorrence of what I had experienced in my dreams.

I was very concerned about these childhood dreams. In my early twenties I consulted a psychologist who said that my childhood dreams meant that I was jealous of my younger brothers and sisters. I was the eldest of four children. She said that as my younger brothers and sisters were born, I was consciously helpful and loving. However, subconsciously I wanted to get rid of them—by throwing them into a furnace. At the time, this sounded as though it could have some basis in truth, and as I wasn't having the nightmares anymore I was content with her answer.

You hear what you need to hear at any given time in your life. You create what you need when you need it. You can't hear things until you are ready to do so.

Last year—more than forty years since my childhood nightmares—I was in London and decided to get a massage. The practitioner was a remarkable man. I felt that when he worked on me he was not only soothing my body but reaching into my soul. Abruptly in the middle of the session he looked at me and said, "You died in Auschwitz."

"Excuse me?" I said.

"You died at Auschwitz."

Shocked, I replied, "I don't think that's the kind of thing that I would forget." (It was also not the sort of thing this man would normally have said to anyone, but somehow he felt impelled to say this to me at that moment.)

I explained to him that as a past-life regressionist, I was familiar with my past lives and would not have forgotten a life as monumental as that. Surprised as I was by his revelation, I was perhaps more surprised by my abrupt, almost rude response.

Very sweetly and humbly he said, "All right . . . maybe I was wrong," and continued the massage. But something shook inside me the way a volcano shakes a mountain at its roots. I thought of my childhood nightmare. I thought of how often people had called me a "Jewish mother"—even though I am not Jewish. I remembered the abject terror I had felt when I arrived at the German border and had to show my papers before entering the country to give some lectures. I thought of the deep compassion I feel for anyone who is unjustly imprisoned.

I walked around in a daze. Was I Jewish in my last life? Did I die at Auschwitz? Why didn't I remember it? Why hadn't I had any visual images? I didn't talk about my experience. My pride as a past-life therapist wouldn't allow me even to consider that I could have had a life in Nazi Germany and forgotten. It was too unbelievable.

A few months later, during a break at a seminar I was giving, a man from Holland talked to me about growing up in that country during the war. He told me about being a young boy when he and his mother were interrogated at length. His mother's papers weren't in order, so she was taken away to a prison camp and he never saw her again.

Suddenly, in a voice seeming not to come from me, I said, "I knew your mother. She was thinking of you before she died. She loved you very, very much." This man and I began to sob uncontrollably. I was stunned by what I had said, because I still hadn't had any memories of being at Auschwitz. Yet, something even deeper than visual images responded to his story. Someplace inside me, I knew that I had spoken the truth. I was there. I did know his mother. And life had come full circle so that the promise I had made to her—to tell her son that she loved him until the end—was fulfilled. The vows we make are extraordinarily powerful, transcending time and space.

Concerned that I still didn't remember a past life in a prison camp, and unable to regress myself back to that time, I began to ask friends about their past lives to see if I could gain any clues. On a subsequent trip to Australia, I had lunch with a woman who had lived with us for three years in Seattle. She, too, was a past-life regressionist. I asked, "Do you remember if you had a lifetime in connection with Nazi Germany?"

She replied, "Oh, I thought you knew. I was a prison warden at Auschwitz. I've always been fascinated by German culture. I studied German and even lived in Germany as a young woman. In fact, as a child I read *Mein Kampf* nine times!"

Suddenly I remembered that this woman used to wear shiny black boots all the time. And I remembered how much I disliked those boots. I began to understand the underlying dynamics of our relationship. I had first met her in New Zealand after a severe fall down a cliffside that damaged my spine. Although we barely knew each other, for the weeks that I was on my back she brought me food and took care of me. I could now see that this was a reenactment of our life together in Auschwitz, where, as a prison guard, she had felt compassion for the prisoners and tried to minister to them. I understood why I had disliked her black boots. Although she was kind to me in the camp, her boots reminded me of all the Nazi officials.

I recently called a very dear family friend who has done extensive regression work and asked him about any connection he might have had with Nazi Germany. He said that he was currently reading a book about Auschwitz. He definitely remembered having been in a concentration camp. In fact, that very night he was planning a pilgrimage to Auschwitz because he felt that he had some unfinished business there. I asked if there was anything in his childhood to give credence to the fact that he had been a prisoner in a concentration camp. He replied that when he was a boy, although he was Christian, he had asked his mother for a Star of David pendant. He remembered his response when asked why he wore it: It was so that he would never forget the great inhumanity that man had done to man.

My friend also mentioned that when he had gone to Germany in his present life, the instant he crossed over the border, his watch stopped, his electric razor didn't work, and he developed a rash. When he left Germany, his watch and shaver worked again and his rash went away. He currently is a volunteer counselor for prisoners. He said he often feels that the prisoners he works with were the Nazi prison wardens in his past life at Auschwitz. His assistance to them now is helping him, and them, to heal old emotional wounds.

At different times in our lives, different past lives and their associated issues become prevalent. At this time in my life I am certain I am dealing with my past life in a concentration camp. There is so much more of the puzzle for me to unfold. I still do not have any visual images or memories, but my body's emotional response is so strong that I know I was there.

I now travel fairly extensively throughout the world. Germany is the only country I visit where attendance at my lectures is limited, and yet I return again and again. It's as if deep inside me is a yearning to forgive the past completely—the past that I can't quite bring myself to remember.

In the coming years you may find an increase in the past-life images that appear in your dreams; therefore, it is important to remember your dreams so these images don't sift gently back into your subconscious.

REMEMBERING YOUR DREAMS

Science has proved that everyone dreams. Even those who swear that they never dream in fact do so. It's just that they don't remember their dreams. Most dreams stay in our consciousness for only ten minutes. For this reason, it is valuable to have a notebook or tape recorder next to your bed so that you can record your dreams immediately, before they fade from memory. Sleep researchers have shown that dreams occur when people are in a very light state at the end of a sleep cycle (a sleep cycle lasts ninety minutes). So, you won't lose sleep by taking time to write down your dreams, because you will be waking at the normal conclusion of a sleep cycle. Using a small flashlight kept next to your bed, rather than turning on the bedroom light, will enable you to go back to sleep more easily after noting the content of your dreams.

Remembering your dreams is like any other skill. As you practice, you will increase your ability to remember. You might want to note the date and time of your dreams to see if a pattern begins to emerge.

PROGRAMMING YOUR DREAMS

As you lie down to go to sleep, take a moment to relax completely. You might begin by slowing down your breath. Take long, slow breaths. Inhale fully. Exhale completely. Changing your breath can change your consciousness.

As you begin to relax, tell yourself, "All thoughts, cares, and concerns are drifting away." Imagine that you are standing beside a slow-moving, shimmering river. Imagine taking your cares one by one and placing them on the river in the kind of leaf-and-stick boats that children make. Watch each one gently float away, taking with it each and every care and concern. This clears your mind of interference, so you can relax even more.

Next, starting with your toes, go through your body, feeling each part relax. For example, breathe into your right foot, hold the breath for a second, then exhale, feeling your right foot become very relaxed. Continue until your entire body feels completely relaxed. Some people report feeling so heavy that they couldn't move if they wanted to; others say that it feels like floating on a cloud.

Once you are completely relaxed, make sure that your spine is straight, then imagine a blue light at the back of your throat and say aloud to yourself, as the spoken word often has greater impact on the subconscious mind: "Tonight I travel to one of my past lives . . . and I remember my dreams." Hold this in mind with as much intensity as you can as you drift off to sleep.

The visualization of a blue light in the throat is an ancient Tibetan technique—although, interestingly, its basis may lie in scientific fact. Modern science has discovered that dreams originate in the brain stem, which lies directly behind the back of the throat. Science has also shown that focusing attention on one part of the anatomy increases the blood circulation to that area. So, putting your attention on the back of your throat can increase the blood flow to the brain stem and thus cause a heightened awareness of dreaming.

When programming your dreams, try to concentrate on one particular area of your life that needs assistance, and focus on that just before you fall asleep. As you are doing the blue-light technique, concentrate on the *feeling* associated with the area that you want to work on in your dreams.

Below are some of the areas on which many people choose to work in their dreams.

PHOBIAS AND FEARS

Fears and phobias often have their source in a past life. Are you so afraid of confronting your boss that your work life is nearly unbearable? Are you constantly anxious about your health? As you fall asleep use the blue light technique and at the same time think about the fear you want to resolve. Take a moment to focus on the physical feelings that your problem causes in your body. Are you breathing quickly, is your stomach tight, is your throat constricted, or do you have a headache? Be aware of physical sensations that accompany your thoughts about the problem. Then imagine that the energy of the blue light is pervading the part (or parts) of your body where the most tension is accumulated. Say aloud to yourself, "Dreams, show me the source of my fear in my past, and lead me to a resolution of all fear." Continue to focus your attention at the back of your throat as you feel the blue light energy gently infusing your whole body and you drift off to sleep.

PHYSICAL AILMENTS AND INJURIES

Sometimes our current physical challenges are symbolic of past-life traumas. For example, someone who has breathing problems may have had a past life in which they suffocated to death. A person with chronic back pain may have had a life in which she felt she could never stand up for herself.

As I described in the section above, place your awareness on the area of your body that is troubling you. If you have many physical problems and the feelings are overwhelming, choose the most intense one. Stay with the feeling for a moment, then imagine the blue light gently entering that part of your body, bringing healing and relief. Say aloud to yourself, "Dreams, reveal to me the source of my discomfort and ailments. Take me back to the time when I first experienced this problem." Hold this thought in the back of your throat, amid the blue light, and gently go to sleep.

RELATIONSHIP DIFFICULTIES

The people to whom you are very close, as well as those with whom you have great difficulty, are likely to have been important to you in other lifetimes (see the section on soulmates in chapter 2). Remembering the dynamics of relationships in other lifetimes and seeing how they affect the way you relate to people in this life can help you to explore completely different ways of being with others. To program your dreams for recollection of these issues, follow the steps described above for dealing with fears and physical ailments. Allow yourself to experience the bodily sensations associated with your difficult relationships. When you are not getting along with someone close to you, what part of your body is most affected? Focus on that part and tell yourself, "My dreams will allow me to remember the significance of this relationship to me in another lifetime, and they will lead me to a wonderful and fulfilling resolution of this issue in my life now."

BLOCKAGES TO CREATIVITY AND ABUNDANCE

Many people create a climate of deprivation for themselves out of a sense of guilt or of a feeling that they don't deserve the good things in life. Often, these feelings seem to have no relation to the circumstances of a person's life. Perhaps you are living your life the best way you can, and have no conscious awareness of any nagging guilt, but you just can't get over the feeling that you don't deserve to have the things you want. Feeling this way leads to a continual poverty consciousness, which prevents you from manifesting abundance in all aspects of your life. Going into the past and locating the source of your feelings of unworthiness can free you from this circle of lack and deprivation. In addition to programming your dreams to release the original past-life blockages, try the following exercise.

Instead of concentrating on the feelings associated with your difficulty, focus on the desired results. For example, if you are having problems with money, imagine the feelings that you would have if you were financially secure. As you lie in bed, form a clear picture of the material things you would like to have, where you would like to travel, and whatever circumstances would allow you to enjoy your life more fully. Just relax and let your mind play at forming these pictures. Enjoy the sights and sounds and smells associated with the things you desire. Then say to yourself, "Tonight when I am sleeping, I will remember where and when I first came to believe that I could not have all that I desire and deserve. Tonight, my dreams will help me to resolve my problems concerning money."

Let this resolve be filled with the pleasure of all the wonderful things you have just envisioned. Push away any feelings of fear and anxiety about what you feel is currently lacking. Let yourself slip off to sleep, secure in the knowledge that these issues will be resolved and that the things you wish for are already in the process of becoming part of your reality. Hold your intention lightly and joyously in the back of your throat as you do the blue-light exercise.

WRITING YOUR DREAMS

As soon as you've had a dream, *immediately* write down what you remember, however insignificant it seems. When you first begin to enter into past lives in your dreams, you might find just a hint of something that appears to be from a past life. Past-life fragments get woven into dreams that seem to be concerned purely with present-life issues. For example, you might dream that you are zooming down a freeway in a red sports car, looking out the window, when you see someone dressed in seventeenth-century clothes. It's as if there's a semipermeable membrane between this life and past ones. Often, at first, just an object or two from a past life will make it through the membrane into your dream. As you become more skillful with your dream states, inner dimensional portals will be made available so that parts or whole scenes will seep through into the present dimension. Eventually you will be able to step through a time traveler's portal so that you are completely immersed in a past life. Until that time, write down everything that you dream. I believe that even the most ordinary dreams have past-life clues woven into them.

ANALYZING YOUR DREAMS

See if there is any similarity between your past-life dreams and your current life. Is there someone in that past life who strikes you as similar to someone in your current life? Notice your emotions in that past life and any decisions or judgments you made. Are any patterns, habits, or fears in that life present now? For example, say you dream of being lost in the snow and are frightened. In your present life you always avoid being out in the snow. This might be a clue to having been lost in the snow in a past life. Remember: One clue isn't enough. You must become a "reincarnation detective" and put all the clues together to get a clear picture.

For example, I recently had a dream that I was in a building with small rooms. Many people were crowded into those rooms and there was a pervading feeling of fear. The major themes were small rooms, crowding, and not feeling safe. I listed these important aspects of the dream. The next step was to look for some correlation in my present life.

At that time we were remodeling our home and the contents of a number of rooms were crowded into just a few. I felt very crowded. In addition, because of the construction work, some of the doors were off their hinges, and perhaps subconsciously, I felt that our home wasn't very safe. This seemed a reasonable explanation for my dream. Then I went to see the film *Schindler's List*, which contains a sequence about Auschwitz. I was astonished to see that the crowded rooms that I had dreamed of only nights before looked almost exactly like the rooms in the Warsaw ghetto into which many Jews were crowded before they were sent to the concentration camps. My dream had a correlation with my present life, but at the same time it provided another clue for me as I continue to explore the life during which I was interned in Auschwitz.

For some people, past lives appear very visually and specifically in their dreams, while others wake up with no visual images but with a feeling. If you have programmed your dreams as I described and you awaken with no specific images, take a moment to notice what you are feeling. If you feel sad, take a moment to expand the sadness into a story. It might go like this: "This sadness feels like the kind that a person would feel if they lost someone very close to them, perhaps a child. It doesn't feel like my child, but someone else's. The child was very carefree and happy. I wish I could have warned this child not to get too close to the waterfall." When you make up your story, don't be overly concerned that it is right. The more that you struggle to be *right*, the more difficult it is for the images to flow from your subconscious.

Write down your stories as well as your memories of your dreams. Sometimes the stories seem to have a life of their own and take shape without any effort. It is very important, however, to do this exercise just as you are waking up. This is the most potent time for your subconscious to give you information about your past. Often people tell me that reviewing their early-morning dream-journal stories, in addition to their dream memories, has allowed the pieces of their reincarnation puzzle to begin to fall into place.

DREAM SEQUENCING AND INTERPRETATION

Another technique for understanding a past-life connection in your dreams is to continue your dream once you are awake. I call this "dream sequencing." To start, set aside twenty to thirty minutes, at any time of day. Find a comfortable chair or bed and make sure that you won't be disturbed. Take a few minutes to relax completely. You can either deepen your breathing or visualize a pleasant scene. Once you are relaxed, let your mind go back into the dream that you recall from the preceding night. Even if it was just a wisp of a dream, it will work for this exercise. Now, replay the dream, just allowing the images to evolve. Don't consciously try to direct the outcome of the scene that is unfolding. Just let your imagination roam freely. A sequence is being formed for your dream.

Don't be concerned if some of the things occurring in the sequence don't seem to make sense—for instance, if a sixteenth-century queen has a crown made of Tupperware. Remember that the language of dreams is symbolic. Your sleeping mind is like an artist weaving together a rich tapestry of images—mixing a bit of this with a bit of that. This is the way it communicates. In order to understand it, you have to let go of your need for everything to fit together in a logical way. Just try to get the *feel* of what the images evoke for you.

Continue allowing the dream sequence to unfold. If at any time you encounter something uncomfortable, surround yourself in an imaginary bubble of safety, or change the series of events so that the sequence resolves itself.

Often, in dreams, people, things, and places have symbolic significance. This is as true for past-life dreams as for those connected mostly with your present life. Jung and other researchers studied the many universal symbols that people all over the world recognize and employ in their art and religion and that show up in their dreams; these are called "archetypal symbols." If you see someone famous in your dream sequence, you might of course have known him or her in another life; but more often the famous person is an archetypal symbol. If Geronimo appears in your dream sequence, it is likely that he represents that part of you that is "strength against all odds."

It can be a challenging task to distinguish which dreams are related to your present life and which are clearly from a past life. Additionally, some people and things appear in dreams literally, as themselves, while others act as symbols for something or someone else. I think the important thing here is to trust your instincts. Your feelings are your best guide to interpreting your dreams. Does the antique chest that looks just like your grandmother's feel as if it has something to do with your present family, or does your heart lead you in an entirely different direction?

When you've completed your dream sequence, write it down in your dream journal. Add it to the clues that you are accumulating.

Dream Process

This process, based on ancient dream techniques, is safe and easy and should be done just before sleep. It's best to record this meditation on a tape and play it back to yourself before you go to bed. Speak with a very slow, relaxed voice. If you like you can substitute "I" for "you" in the meditation. You might want to include some background music. (Remember, always keep your dream journal next to your bed to record your dreams.)

Allow your body to assume a restful position, making sure your spine is straight. You may do this now. Good.

Now begin to take very easy, deep breaths . . . nice and easy breaths. Inhale and exhale. That's good. It's almost as if you are being breathed in and out. It's as if nothing else exists except for your breath. In and out. All your thoughts and cares are drifting away as you continue to breathe in and out. With each breath, you find yourself relaxing more and more. You find yourself moving deeper and deeper within yourself. Imagine that you are flowing into your body as you inhale . . . and out of your body as you exhale. In and out. Each breath takes you deeper. It is as if you are drifting with the very gentle ebb and flow of the universe and your breath is connecting you to that rhythm, that harmony. Breathe gently and evenly as you continue your journey into a very relaxed, yet aware, state. Allow your awareness to drift gently into your body and allow yourself to be aware of any tightness. Just notice it. Good.

Feel that tightness just melting away like ice melting on a warm summer afternoon. That's good. Drifting and floating. Drifting and floating. Now allow your imagination to begin to drift and float. Just imagine, in your mind's eye, a moonlit night. There's a beautiful full moon and you are walking along the sandy seashore. Ahead, washed in moonlight, is a bed. It is luxurious and voluptuous. The pillows are soft and round and firm. Take some time to imagine this bed, making it as real as possible. Make it your perfect bed. Really imagine this bed.

Now, slowly and ever so sensuously, crawl into this bed. Be aware of the opulent plumpness of the pillows. Feel the silky smoothness of the sheets as you slide easily between them. It feels so good to be in this bed. Fanned by the gentle sounds and cadence of the sea, as the tides ebb and flow, you find yourself drifting off into a deeeep, deeeep sleeeep.

Now put your awareness in your present body. Feel the sensation of the sheets on your skin. Be aware of your head on your pillow. Allow yourself to be aware of the sounds of the night. Listen to the sounds of your body. As you listen to the sound of your breath, know that tonight is a special night. Somewhere in the magic of the night, a metamorphosis will occur. You know that you will be gently transported back to another place . . . another time. You will be taken back to one of your past lives. You know that a door to the past will make itself evident in your dreams. As your body sleeps, your spirit will travel through time and space, dancing through the stars and touching past incarnations.

Now imagine that you are going forward in time, to the time when you are about to wake up. Your dreams are still very evident. Imagine that, without losing your dream images, you are rolling over and writing down those dreams—dreams that hold the key to your past life.

You may now either return to conscious awareness or drift off to sleep.

You can repeat this exercise again and again. I wish you well on your inner journeys.

6. RESOLUTIONS: HOW TO HEAL PAST-LIFE BLOCKAGES DURING REGRESSION

Once a person has entered into a past life, whether in dreams or while awake, it is not uncommon to discover something uncomfortable that needs resolution. One of the main benefits of past-life regression is that it can finally free you of the hindrances that have been blocking you through many lifetimes. However, you first need to learn exactly how to accomplish this. This chapter contains a number of simple exercises that you can do alone or with someone with whom you feel safe. (I suggest you try several or all of the exercises to find out which ones work best for you.)

Feel It

People have often asked me, "What if I do the processes and come up with a lifetime that is scary—or I have a past-life nightmare?" Instead of shutting down these emotions, *choose* to feel them. When you do this, the fear will dissipate. For example, when you go to a horror movie, you pay to be scared;

you go out of your way to create a scary experience for yourself. When you have paid the attendant for the roller coaster ride and you are absolutely terrified, remember it was *you* who rushed to join the line.

Don't be afraid of the emotions that you might feel when you get in touch with a past life. No one would go to hear a symphony if only one note was to be played. A symphony needs to have thousands of notes—high points and low. Life is like that. So enjoy all your emotions. Each one is like a precious note in a symphony. As you experience a past life, relish and explore each emotion that arises.

If you find yourself stuck in an emotion, don't deny it or try to get rid of it; instead, move toward it and let it embrace you. See yourself turning around and letting it flow all around you. Exaggerate it. For example, if you discover a lifetime where you were devastated by the death of your lover, instead of trying not to feel that sadness or repressing it—which is what you did at the time—let yourself feel even sadder.

Go into the center of that sadness and feel it. Find the spot in your body where that sadness resides and allow yourself to experience it. This will help you start to release issues that have been creating barriers for you.

The emotions that you repress stay with you lifetime after lifetime and create blockages in your life, so it's important to experience your emotions. However, there is a difference between *dramatizing* your emotions and *experiencing* them. When I began doing past-life therapy seminars, many people during the processes began crying or sobbing, sometimes very dramatically. I assumed this was important to the ultimate positive results that they achieved. However, when I did a past-life seminar in Vancouver, Canada, and nobody cried uncontrollably, I was distraught, thinking that the seminar hadn't worked. I was then astonished to receive many letters claiming positive results from the participants of that seminar. I assumed it was a fluke, but the same thing occurred in my next seminar and has occurred ever since. Very few people become emotionally fraught in my seminars, yet very dramatic positive results are reported. As I began to investigate this phenomenon, I realized that instead of externalizing and dramatizing their emotions, people were going to the source of their emotions and truly feeling them. Sometimes, dramatizing your emotions can actually keep you separate from them. I met a woman who had been crying hard almost every day for twenty years over the death of her husband. When she went inside her body to the source of her sadness, she was able to grieve truly for the first time in twenty years. She then "experienced" her grief instead of externalizing it and was able to release it completely. By finding the place in your body where the emotion exists and going into the emotion, you can remove it at its roots.

Here is an exercise that you can do if you begin to feel any uncomfortable emotions during your past-life regressions. It is similar to the exercise called Locate the Body Sensation in chapter 4, although that exercise is aimed at recalling a past life. This exercise allows you to release emotions once they have occurred during your past-life recall.

Emotion-Release Exercise

Begin by traveling through your body to locate the unwanted emotion. There is always a sensation in your body associated with that emotion. For example, your chest might feel constricted during sadness and your shoulders might tighten during anger. However, not everyone associates the same body sensations with the same emotions.

Once you have located the emotion you are feeling, focus your entire attention on that part of your body and *intensify* the sensation. For example, if you feel a constriction in your chest, make it tighter. Feel it more. As you do so, notice what shape the emotion/sensation seems to be. For example, the constriction in the chest associated with sadness might seem pear-shaped, with the smaller end of the pear pointing down. As you continue to focus on your chest, notice how big the sensation is. The pear might seem about six inches wide and eight inches long. Then notice if it has a color. (It is not mere coincidence that people associate certain colors with certain emotions: "She's in the pink"; "He's feeling blue"; "I'm having a black day"; "He saw red.")

Continue to ask yourself these questions:

- What body sensation am I feeling that is associated with this emotion? (Sometimes the sensation will shift to another spot in the body. Follow the sensation wherever it goes.)
- If the sensation had a shape, what shape would it be?
- If the sensation had a size, what size would it be?
- If the sensation had a color, what color would it be?

Continue to intensify what you are feeling. Often the color, shape, size, and location change as you are doing this; just continue to move into your emotions. Often, doing this exercise alone is enough to begin to release the uncomfortable emotions that arose during your past-life experiences. Sometimes, when you do this exercise, memories from another past life will emerge spontaneously. Just as a temper tantrum thrown at age twenty may be the result of a temper tantrum thrown under similar circumstances at age three, so the past-life trauma that you are working with may have its source in another, similar lifetime. So don't be surprised if you find yourself catapulted from one past life to another. It is beneficial, because you are going even closer to the source of your present-life difficulty.

Detach from It

If you find yourself in a situation that holds very uncomfortable emotions, imagine that you are floating above the scene. Just observe it. Detach yourself from the particular view that you held at the time. A technique that I often suggest is to play the incident through at high speed, like an old Charlie Chaplin film. Then run the incident backward at high speed. For example, if you find yourself running and falling off a cliff, see yourself running and falling very fast and then see yourself flipping up off the ground, soaring back to the top of the cliff, and then running backward! This exercise can take some of the emotional trauma out of the event and help you to detach from it.

When you detach from a situation, you can observe it from a greater, more objective perspective. Beryl experienced a lifetime in which her husband died of an infection that he got while working in their garden. In her regression she felt tremendous sadness tinged with guilt over her loss. The sadness was for the loss of her husband; the guilt was for the fact that she had been capable of doing the garden work but told her husband she wasn't strong enough to do it. Though of course it was not her fault, she felt guilty, and the guilt had permeated her present life. When she detached from the scene and floated above it to gain an expanded perspective, she saw that her intense love for her husband in that life was sometimes to the detriment of her children. She often put aside her children's needs in order to spend more time with her husband. After his death, she began to nurture her children more and give them the attention and love that they needed. When she detached from the scene, she came to peace about her husband's death and understood that everything has a purpose, even if we don't understand it at the time.

When you detach from a scene, you can float above it or you can watch it as if you were watching a movie. If it is very traumatic, you can watch yourself watching the scene as a way of further detaching from the situation.

Another way to detach from an uncomfortable past life is to make it seem silly. A client came to me who had always felt intimidated by men. She was a mature, responsible woman, but as soon as she was near a man, she began to act in a meek, childlike way. Having regressed to a life in which she had a very strict, disciplinarian father, she saw that whenever she was with men, she activated the memory of being a meek little girl from that past life. In her past-life exploration she arrived at a point where her father was giving her a very stern dressing-down. I told her to imagine him standing in front of her in red spotted pants and with a silly hat on his head, then to imagine people walking by and laughing. Suddenly she, too, was laughing, and she was no longer a meek little girl. This session completely changed her attitude to men.

Detaching from a past-life scene helps you to understand that every lifetime you have allows you to grow—and that every experience is important for your evolution as a soul. I believe that Spirit is interested not so much in your comfort as in your personal growth, even if it means going through difficult, painful experiences.

Change It

I find the most powerful technique to resolve an uncomfortable past-life issue is to change the circumstances of that life until it feels comfortable or enjoyable. I believe that you can actually change the past. If this is too far-fetched for you to accept, then imagine that you are changing the images that are stored in your brain. As you change those images, imagine you are changing the associated limiting beliefs.

Remember the example of Joshua, the young man whose friends chased him into the ravine when they thought he was ridiculing the king? Imagine that he changes this past-life memory. He stops running and stands his ground. Those who were chasing him stop. There's a standoff. Then everyone bursts out laughing. Changing his mental image of being hurt to one of speaking his mind changes the previous inner belief that he had developed. When his limiting belief changes, his life changes. A man who feels that if he speaks the truth he will be punished will create circumstances to validate his subconscious belief. Physical matter coalesces around us based on our subconscious beliefs. Change your subconscious beliefs, and the world around you will seem to change.

The following letter, sent to me after a past-life seminar, shows the power of changing your past-life memories.

> I would like to share with you, Denise, a past life that I became aware of during your weekend past-life workshop, which has had an enormous impact on my life now. In my present life my son was born with the umbilical cord around his neck and has always been a screamer. He also had a speech pattern where he would repeat several words in the

sentence many times. He is now three and a half years old and an example of his type of speech is as follows: "The cat, cat, cat, cat is running running very, very, very, very fast fast."

The past life I experienced in your Journeys into Past Lives seminar was a life where my son and I both were American Indians. I was my [current] son's mother and he was about eleven years old. My son and I were separated from our tribe and we were attacked by another tribe. [In the past-life regression] I was facing several of the attackers. It became clear to me that they were going to kill me and torture my son. I became very angry and tried to convince them to leave my son alone. When it became clear that this wasn't working, I turned to my son and we both looked deeply into each other's eyes. My son, in an instant, understood what I was going to do, we both screamed, and I strangled him.

I don't know why but I wasn't killed and I lived the rest of my lifetime with the anguish of having killed my son. During the regression, I changed the outcome (as you suggested). I saw many images of beautiful crystals and total safety and wonderful open, clear communication between us. For me this was very exciting.

It became even more exciting when, after the seminar, I returned to pick up my son from my mother's and she proceeded to tell me that at one point during the weekend my son had gone into the bedroom and begun to sob and sob. The sobbing continued for nearly thirty minutes . . . he couldn't seem to stop. This happened at the exact same time as I was getting in touch with our life together as Indians.

I am writing this just one week later and my son has

> stopped the word repetitions in his sentences and his screaming has subsided. I used to be so wound up by his screaming that I wanted to put my hands around his neck. Although I never did, the urge to do so was very strong—almost overwhelming.
>
> This regression has been a major turning point for both my son and myself. I feel really excited and empowered as a result of the weekend. Thank you for a most special weekend.

By changing the circumstances of a past life that she and her son were reliving, not only did she change the way that she felt about her son, she changed his behavior as well!

Here is another letter sent to me that shows the value of changing the circumstances of a traumatic past life:

> I was one of the several hundred people at your Past Life Seminar in Sydney in November. You may remember me as the woman who gave you a book during the seminar. My reason for writing is to tell you about the incredible occurrences that have happened over the last few days since your seminar.
>
> When my husband and his first wife divorced eleven years ago it was very bitter and he was stopped from seeing his children, in particular the youngest child, who was seven years old at the time. My husband is a very special person and this has been hard on him.
>
> During one of the weekend's regressions, I concentrated on the thought that if I had been a part of my husband's family in a past life, I wanted some insight and under-

standing. Well, I'm still not sure exactly what my role was in the past life that I experienced, except that I saw that I was comforting an old man who was dying. He wasn't dying of old age but of a broken heart, blaming himself for the death by drowning of his three children. I saw that the old man was my present-day husband. You told us we could change what was upsetting so I changed the situation. It was in the future in that life and *I* was dying and the old man and his three children were comforting me. They were very close and very happy. This apparently had an effect on the present! Today the youngest child, seemingly out of the clear blue, called and is coming to visit tomorrow. This is the most hopeful thing to have occurred in eleven years! Last night I told my husband of the regression and though he is skeptical, he is open-minded. Wow! So thank you, Denise. Isn't life grand when you know that love is all that matters?

This example shows that even if you aren't aware of all the details of your past life, just changing the circumstances can have a very empowering effect on your present life.

Here is an example from my life that shows the step-by-step mechanics of how to change past-life memories.

When my daughter, Meadow, was younger, I asked her if I could try a new relaxation technique on her before I tried it on my clients. I needed to hold her wrist, but as I did so she said, "Mom, you know I don't like to have my wrists touched. In fact I can't even look at my wrists because when I see the veins I get squeamish." I hadn't been aware of this before, but proceeded with the relaxation process.

Once she was relaxed, I thought I would take the opportunity to see if I could get to the source of her difficulty. I said,

"Imagine a situation that might relate to your wrists." (Children, incidentally, are very easy to regress into past lives. Adults usually develop a buffer to their intuition, making it more difficult to be regressed.)

"Mom, I see a desert. I live in the desert."

"Are you male or female?"

"I'm a young man. I have a religious belief that I feel very strongly about. It's a good belief. I want to tell everyone about it. I know it will help them. . . . I'm now in a small village to tell everyone about this new belief. They don't want to know about it. In fact they are getting very angry. Oh, no!"

"What is it?"

"They're tying me up. They've cut my wrists. I'm watching the blood slowly flow out of my body. I'm tied up, so I can't stop it."

"You can change this experience," I told her. "You can replay it but give it a positive outcome."

"Okay. I'm replaying it. . . . I've traveled across the desert to tell the villagers about my new religion. Everyone who greets me is happy to meet me. Everyone seems really interested in talking to me and finding out about my beliefs. When I leave the village I've made many good friends."

"How do you feel?"

"I feel great. It feels good to know that I can really tell people how I feel."

All this occurred in about twenty minutes. My daughter came back from her experience feeling refreshed and rejuvenated. I asked her to look at the veins on her wrists. She said she was amazed that she could now look at them without feeling queasy.

Up until that point she had always been very hesitant to say how she truly felt about anything. But now a remarkable thing occurred: she began to tell people how she felt, to share her personal point of view. This was something she had never done before. The Gulf War broke out soon afterward and Meadow called the fifty students in her class to ask them to march against the war with her. Some students agreed with her, while others vehemently disagreed. She felt strongly about the war and was willing to let other people know how she felt. To me, this was a minor miracle. I believe that our one twenty-minute session made all the difference.

Some people are concerned that if they change the past, they will negatively affect the present. They'll ask, "What if I change the past and then my mother never meets my father. Will I still exist?" Such questions are interesting to me philosophically, but in my experience, changing a traumatic past life always has a positive effect on everyone. It seems to me that when you clear an emotional blockage from your energy field, you create a resonance that positively and deeply affects you and others. I believe that you *can* change the past. Just changing the images in your brain associated with limiting beliefs has a positive and empowering effect on life.

See It from Another Viewpoint

A technique for resolving past-life situations that involve another person is to imagine that you are jumping into the awareness or the body of that person. See the entire situation from his point of view. When you do this, you almost always forgive the other's actions, because you recognize that if you were in his place you would react in the same way.

Although I definitely don't condone the actions of the man

who shot me, it was enormously helpful for me to imagine that I was in his consciousness. I felt that he couldn't stop himself from killing people, in much the same way as addicts cannot control their cravings. Seeing life through his eyes made it much easier for me to forgive him. This was valuable for me, because resentment was eating away at me.

Another interesting example is the case of Charles. He had been quarreling with his younger brother seemingly since his brother was born. The quarreling had continued into adulthood and their arguments were having a negative effect on the entire family, as each brother tried to get other family members to agree with his point of view. Charles became aware that these altercations were becoming increasingly counterproductive and affecting many areas of his life. He attended a past-life workshop I gave in New Zealand and recalled a life in which he was an accounting clerk in Denmark and his present-life brother was his demanding and argumentative employer. In the regression he took my suggestion of seeing the world through his employer's eyes. Instantly he understood that his employer had very severe back pain that made his every move painful. Because of his severe pain he was continually in a foul mood and treated his employees very badly.

With this new understanding, Charles began to have compassion for his employer/brother. (It's interesting to note that his brother in his present life had a back injury.) Charles reported that he saw his brother a few days after the seminar and was astonished to find that there was much less animosity between them. Their relationship has continued to grow closer.

Working through past-life blockages is one of the most rewarding kinds of work you can do. Many of my clients have reported a greater sense of exhilaration and joy than they had ever experienced before. But it can be a rough and rocky road while you are in the process. Share your pain with someone who cares about you, or seek professional help if you think you need it, and know that what awaits you is more than worth it. Freed of the bindings that have been keeping you down, you will finally be able to soar to the heights you have always dreamed of!

7.
SPIRIT GUIDES, ANGELS, AND PAST LIVES

We all have guides, whether we consciously know it or not, and those who communicate with their guides have an enormous wealth of resources to tap in to. Guides come to us from the world of Spirit. They hold a unique perspective of the universe, creation, life, and eternal love. Nonphysical beings or entities that give guidance, assistance, and love can be teachers or protectors as well as helpers to direct our paths and to release old karma. They remind us of the world beyond the here and now. Guides can be of great value in gaining access to your past lives.

People may have multiple guides over a lifetime. Guides may enter during our critical life passages or stay with us consistently over a long period. Guides have their own personalities, goals, perspectives, and styles of communication. A guide may appear in the quiet of meditation or arrive as an unseen, loving presence that you feel around you as you go about your everyday activities. Your guide may appear to you in a daydream, or in a dream at night—as a person dressed in period clothes, or as an animal. A guide can arrive as a feeling, a smell, a light, a sound, or even just a sense of knowing that it is present.

I believe that guides are actual spiritual beings who exist on higher planes of consciousness and are working to help us in our evolution. Your guides are usually beings who have been with you in other lives and have completed their earth plane existence; they are now in the spirit world, assisting you with your life's journey.

However, some people view guides not as spiritual entities with consciousness outside of themselves but as part of themselves. They feel that guides are their higher self personified. Although they regard guides as a way to access their intuition, they feel that their guides are actually a part of themselves that they are not normally in touch with. Psychologists usually share this view, explaining that guides are aspects of ourselves that we haven't yet "owned" or integrated into our personalities.

I don't believe that these two points of view are mutually exclusive. I don't believe there is anything "out there" that *isn't* you. The spiritual beings are you, just as the sky and the sea and the stars are you. I believe that each person in our lives, whether or not he or she has a physical body, represents an aspect of ourselves. In a larger sense, each person in my life is a part of me. Whatever the reality, many past-life therapists find it enormously valuable to work with guides—they report that it is much easier to connect with past lives if they first connect their patient with his or her guide. I have heard this view consistently from past-life therapists around the world.

What Do Guides Do?

When you have a problem and suddenly a solution seems to come out of nowhere, that is often the mark of a guide's intervention. Moments of inspiration can be the result of a guide's assistance. Those times when you are feeling down and then suddenly feel uplifted—again, for no apparent reason—can also indicate a guide's intercession. Guides can assist creativity, abundance, and healing, and can help harmonize difficult relationships. They also can help you with cultivating personal qualities such as forgiveness, acceptance, and love. They can be your protectors and help you avoid dangerous situations. Guides can even help with mundane issues such as getting parking spaces, finding lost property, or choosing the right clothes to wear. Guides can also help you connect with your past lives.

In addition to assisting the past-life recall processes, one of the primary reasons for guide contact is to allow a deepening of the understanding that there are dimensions beyond our physical, earthly existence. They give a more expansive view beyond our humanity and can be a source of spiritual inspiration.

Not so commonly known, however, is that in return for these gifts from the "other side" we offer a great deal to these guides. Just as we are evolving and growing, so are our guides. They evolve and grow through working with us, sometimes through several lifetimes.

Information from Guides

Traditional metaphysics holds the belief that if a spirit says something, it must be true. I don't agree with that. I believe that just because someone dies, he doesn't automatically become the sage on the mountain. If he was a couch potato when he was alive, he will most certainly be a couch potato when he is dead.

There are entities on the other side that are desperate to communicate, and they will chatter endlessly, regardless of whether their information is worthwhile or even accurate. There are entities that are no wiser or clearer than any of your neighbors. For example, although you might value the opinion of your neighbor, you wouldn't necessarily drop everything and move to Tahiti if she told you to. When a guide gives you advice, it is quite all right to question it and even reject it. It is important to realize that guides, like friends, have opinions and personality quirks. These discarnate beings don't even necessarily agree with one another. If you compare the testimony of different guides channeled through mediums, you will find that they very rarely agree.

Test any information against your own inner knowing. If it is useful, then take it as your own. If not, let it go. The important thing to remember is that *you* are making the choice—and ultimately *you* are responsible for the outcome of all the choices you make.

Guides are effective sources of advice; however, it is easy to become too dependent on them, to fall into the trap of asking their advice on every aspect of your life. Valuable though guides are, it is an important part of your evolution to be able to step beyond them and rely on your own inner knowing. When you do this, you are connecting with your higher self—that part of you that continues after the body is sloughed off. Your higher self is your direct connection to Spirit, or God.

Types of Guides

There are many kinds of guides. Remember that like attracts like, so your guides will always reflect an aspect of yourself—though this is not always obvious. I know of one instance where a tough woman who taught self-defense was surprised to find that her guide was very soft and feminine. She was expecting a Viking or at least a samurai warrior. She realized that her guide came to offer balance in her life. In the same way, someone who is very disorganized and flamboyant may get a librarian-type guide—again, to offer balance.

Guides can also be angels. Although these heavenly ambassadors are excellent conveyors of universal love, they are not always equipped to deal with earthly problems. People who come from cultures that honor the spirits of ancestors will often be presented with ancestors as guides.

Remember, it is not the form that the guide takes, or the manner of communication, that is important. The importance lies in the value the information has to you. Once you have established a relationship with your guides, you might notice a distinct feeling when they are nearby. Sometimes it is like a tingling sensation in a certain part of the body. For instance, Ann's little finger tingles when her guide is present. Rachel's body will sway to and fro as a "yes" answer from her guide, and side to side if her guide is saying "no." Some people hear their own name spoken, or become aware of a distinctive smell when the guide is close at hand. One man's guide came from a past life in Eastern Europe—his presence was always accompanied by a distinct smell of sauerkraut. I get a tingling feeling between my shoulder blades when my master guide has something to say. Some people hear their guide speak, others get distinct visual images, and yet others just get a sense of what their guide is trying to communicate. The important thing is to begin to develop the sensitivity to be aware of communications from your guides.

MASTER GUIDE OR LIFETIME GUIDE

I have attended numerous births, and there is usually a point at which an influx of energy can be felt. This can be the influence of the birthing guides that are in attendance, but more often it represents the arrival of the master guide. This is a guide who sometimes will stay with you for an entire lifetime. However, if there is a change in life direction or emphasis, the master guide may step back and other guides will come forward.

Often, children report having an invisible friend. I believe that this unseen, imaginary friend is a guide. The master guide assumes an identity with which the child can communicate as he develops. It's important to allow your child to have that "friend" and not to discourage him or her or to deny the existence of the relationship. Especially in early childhood, the master guide is there as an ally or godparent, watching over, protecting, and loving the child.

When I was a child, every night just before bed I was aware that there was someone with me. I never saw this individual, but I felt a wonderful, loving presence near me. This didn't seem unusual to me—it was as natural as breathing. As I got older, the loving presence visited me less and less. I believe that that being was my master guide, watching over me and protecting me during the night.

SPECIAL-PURPOSE GUIDES

Although some guides are lifelong companions, others come to work with you in one particular area. For example, in my healing work, a Native American guide assists me only while I am actually working with an individual. I have another guide who helps me with questions about diet. Artists and musicians very often have guides who help with creativity.

A special-purpose guide may help you develop a particular quality, such as patience or perseverance or abundance. I have a special guide who helps me just with my dreams—to program, remember, and understand them—and another who assists me with past-life awareness. There can even be specialty guides to help you with something as ordinary as shopping. I have a wonderful, voluptuous, redheaded shopping guide who wears dozens of dangling bracelets, dresses outrageously from head to foot, and speaks with a thick accent. When I'm at my wit's end shopping and can't find what I need, she comes right in and—presto!—I find the perfect item.

SHORT-TERM GUIDES

Sometimes a guide will arrive for just a short period of time. For example, I was in New Mexico doing healing work with a man who had just been in a traumatic automobile accident. Just as I was about to begin, an old Pueblo Indian woman guide came through and gave me unusual but specific information on how to work with my patient. I had never seen this guide before and have never seen her since. But I took her advice—with excellent results.

Later that day I spent time with Dancing Feather. I asked him about the advice that had been given, because it was so unusual. He said that the information given was very accurate according to Native American ways. (Now deceased, Dancing Feather occasionally comes to me as a guide and often appears to those who attend my seminars.)

Sometimes these guides, such as the old Indian woman, appear only in a particular location. I was attending a festival in a coastal village in Madeira, an island off the coast of Morocco. We were enjoying the warm evening as we strolled along the seawall. Suddenly a terrified, shawl-clad woman appeared holding an unconscious child. The child had fallen headfirst from the seawall and was barely breathing. The nearest doctor was hours away. The frightened mother looked to us to help and put her child in my arms. I called for guide assistance. A guide who wore the vestments of a Catholic priest came, and within minutes the child was conscious and playing. This guide was never seen again; apparently he was indigenous to that area.

If you are interested in accessing your past lives, short-term guides may appear spontaneously or at your request to help you. They will often present themselves in your dreams. Guides also come in for a short period during an emotionally or physically traumatic time.

PAST-LIFE GUIDES

Usually your guides are those with whom you have shared a past life. A guide may be someone who taught you or gave you guidance or someone for whom you felt a deep love. Guides appear in many forms. However, guides will often appear in a form that is familiar to you from a past life that you shared. For instance, if you had a life in a convent in the south of France in the seventeenth century, you might find that your guide was the abbess and dresses accordingly.

I became interested in past-life guides because of a phenomenon that occurred spontaneously again and again during regressions with my clients. A guardian figure would appear in the inner explorations, sometimes wearing period clothes. Sometimes it would come as a light or a sound or a symbol, and sometimes even as an animal. There was always a wonderful, loving, protective feeling that accompanied these guides.

Our inner journeys seem to allow guardian beings from past lives to surface. Not only do they appear spontaneously for people who are being regressed, but they appear in other inner voyages. People who have had near-death experiences often report that they were guided by very protective, loving spiritual entities. Meditators and even individuals who spend time in isolation tanks report seeing guides and guardians from the past. Perhaps it is when we take the time to be still and turn our awareness inward that their presence can be felt most strongly.

PRESENT-LIFE GUIDES

At times your guide will be someone whom you knew in your current life but who has died, such as a grandparent or other person whom you cared for as a child. I find this very often in my regression work with clients. There is an emotional connection between the individual and the guide that goes beyond time and space. Although the essence of the deceased stays the same, sometimes their personality changes when they are in the spirit world. My Cherokee grandmother was very stoic and quiet when she was alive; she carried herself with the dignified demeanor of an Indian elder and was reserved with all her grandchildren. Although I respected her, she wasn't the kind of grandmother with whom you wanted to cuddle. I was therefore surprised when, one day many years after her death, she appeared in my dreams to give me guidance. Gone was the stern gaze, and in its place was a wondrous, glowing Indian face filled with warmth, peace, quietness, and grace. I continue to feel her presence from time to time both in my dreams and in my waking life.

A guide can also be someone who is still alive. The very first time I attempted to contact a guide, I saw a statuesque woman in her fifties who radiated magnificence. Two weeks later I went for my first Rolfing session—a type of massage. When the door swung open, I was astonished to be greeted by the exact image of the woman I had seen in my meditation. Over the next few months, as her sturdy fingers kneaded my muscles, this lovely woman healed my body and soul. At that time in my life she was indeed a guide to me. Although she wasn't consciously aware of it, her higher self was my guide. With the exception of a guru, living guides are not usually aware of the service that they render. When you dream about someone you know in this life helping you in some way, often that person's higher self is actually assisting and guiding you.

Guides are different from ghosts. A ghost is basically someone who has died and hasn't fully realized or accepted it. A ghost is still on the earth plane—but without a body—and may be confused, sad, or angry. It's important to understand that ghosts cannot hurt you. When people have difficulty with ghosts, they aren't harmed by them but have been shaken by their own fears. Ghosts are at a great disadvantage because they no longer have a body. The kindest thing to do if you encounter a ghost is to talk to him or her as you would anyone who is confused or unhappy. Let him know that he should go to the Light. Be gentle but firm.

SPIRIT ANIMAL GUIDE

The use of totems (also called animal guides, power animals, or spirit animals) in native cultures is well documented. Members of these cultures believe that each person has an animal spirit that can give assistance and strength—it is personal "medicine." There can be one animal or more assisting at any point in time, although usually there is one major totem that is influencing, guiding, and teaching.

Totems often appear in meditations and past-life regressions as guides for those who have had past lives in native cultures. However, anyone from any culture can benefit from accessing his or her animal guide.

Each spirit animal has its own qualities and abilities. By communing with one particular totem, you gain access to its qualities. Although the meanings ascribed to particular power animals can vary according to the particular culture, there are some similarities. Often a person with the bear totem will be a good healer and have the introspection of a bear, but will be challenged to come out of the cave. Those with a deer totem may be involved with people, interrelating with others, and may be very fertile in life. They may also have a gentle nature like a deer and sometimes need protection for themselves from hunters, as some people may prey on them. People with the eagle totem often see into other dimensions and have ESP abilities, yet often find themselves alone.

There are a number of ways in which you can find your power animal. It may come to you repeatedly in dreams or meditation. Or you may recognize it by observing the animals to which you are drawn. Sometimes a personal totem may be your favorite animal since childhood. A power animal may come to you in unusual ways. For example, if an owl's feather drops at your feet as you walk in the woods, there is a good chance that the owl is one of your totems. If a particular animal appears to you again and again in different forms it may be your totem. For example, if you feel particularly drawn to a painting that features horses, and then someone sends you a photograph of a horse, and then horses start to appear in your dreams, there is a good chance that the horse is your spirit animal guide.

Observing the attributes of particular animals is also helpful in discovering your totem. For example, bears wake up slowly in the morning and tend to be creatures of habit. If you leap out of bed in the morning full of energy to start your day and tend to vary your activities, it is unlikely that the bear is your totem. Learning the characteristics of various animals and comparing them with your personality can be helpful in finding your totem. Your power animal can bring an understanding of your strengths as well as assist you in times of distress. You can communicate with your totem animal in much the same way as you communicate with a guide that takes a human form.

As we move into a time when planetary consciousness is focused on contributing to the healing and understanding of the earth, the value of animal totems increases. Accessing with your animal totem, even if you haven't had past lives in native cultures, will help you unite with the earth. This is healing for all.

The following meditation is designed to assist you in connecting with your animal guide. You can read this meditation into a tape recorder to play back to yourself just before you go to sleep, or you can do it with a friend, who reads the meditation to you. Remember, if you read the meditation into a tape recorder, substitute "you" with "I," so the meditation is in first person.

Animal Guide Meditation

Start by relaxing. When you are deeply relaxed you can connect with your guides and spirit helpers and totems. Just sit or lie comfortably in a quiet place and become aware of your breathing. Stop for a moment and monitor the shallowness or deepness of your breath. Then take a full, deep breath and fill your abdomen so that it expands like a balloon. Keep holding your breath, longer and longer . . . hold . . . hold . . . and then just let it out very slowly, easily, and gently. . . . Repeat this exercise. Fill up your abdomen and allow it to expand . . . hold that breath . . . hold . . . hold and then release . . . let it go. Now take two shallow breaths, and feel the difference in your body between breathing deeply and breathing shallowly. Then allow your breath to flow in a natural, effortless way for a few moments. . . . Good.

Now focus your attention again on the area of your abdomen. With each breath, feel yourself expanding and contracting. Really feel the air entering you . . . feel your body expand. As your breathing becomes more rhythmic, turn your attention to the oxygen entering through your nostrils. Visualize yourself breathing in the purest, cleanest, healthiest air. Give this air a color, and see that color radiating down deep inside the cavity of your lungs, oxygenating and revitalizing all the parts that it reaches. Imagine that the oxygen you are breathing is healing and regenerating your lungs and your entire circulatory system. . . . Aaah, that feels so good!

Now allow yourself to slip down to an even deeper level of relaxation. Keep your attention on your breathing. Another deep breath . . . hold it . . . and exhale. Let it go slowly, and let out a gentle sigh . . . mmmmm . . . that feels so relaxing and calming. Your body is feeling rested; all cares and tensions are just fading away.

With your next breath, focus your consciousness in your legs. Visualize your legs as empty vessels, and now fill those vessels with breath. See and feel the whole area around your legs being filled with a pure, cleansing breath. As you slowly exhale, feel your legs become heavier and heavier . . . sinking into the floor beneath you. They feel incredibly relaxed, and the muscles become more and more free of tension. Your deep breaths allow your body to relax with freedom and ease.

Take another long, deep breath and fill your hips and buttocks. As you exhale, feel those powerful muscles relaxing and letting go. Good. Now move your awareness up and breathe into your entire torso area, filling your lungs and back and chest and shoulders with breath. Hold . . . Hold . . . Hold . . . Now exhale completely. Good. Your entire torso is now completely relaxed.

As if you were filling up a long balloon, breathe into your right arm. When you exhale, feel your arm relax and let go. Feel it becoming very, very relaxed and heavy. Now breathe into your left arm and let go. Good. Now breathe into your neck and head. Fill your entire neck and head with your breath, and when you exhale let all thoughts, cares, and concerns just drift away. Just drift away. Good. Now your entire body is relaxed and feeling good. Continue with nice, full, easy breaths. Be conscious of the oxygen filling and being released from your lungs. In and out. In and out. There is a rhythm, a cadence, to the universe. At this moment your breath is aligning with that rhythm. You are breathing in harmony with all the patterns and rhythms of life. Really feel and imagine and be aware of this. You have a brief time to do so.

Now that you are completely relaxed, you can begin an inward journey that will assist you in finding your animal guide. In your imagination, travel to a beautiful place in nature. You can imagine a place that you have been before where you felt very comfortable and good, or you can travel to a place that exists in your imagination. If you have difficulty visualizing this beautiful location, just get the feeling of it. Feel how good it would be to find yourself in this lovely place. Get a sense of the freshness of the air and the strength of the earth beneath you. Take a moment really to imagine yourself in this beautiful place in nature. [If you are making a tape, you might leave some space here.] Imagine as you are in this place in nature that you are feeling very healthy and well. Good. Now find a place to sit down—it might be on a boulder or a tree stump or a sand dune—and make yourself comfortable.

As you are sitting, imagine that a mist is beginning to form. The mist becomes thicker and thicker until you cannot see anything around you. As you sit in this mist, your intuition—your sixth sense—is expanding. Although you cannot see anything, you can feel the approach of your spirit animal. You can feel the strength and the wildness and the power of your totem. Closer and closer. Reach out now into the mists and touch your animal helper. Do you seem to be touching fur, feathers, reptilian scales, or something wet, like a sea creature? At the moment of your touch there is instant rapport between you and your totem. As the mists clear, you can see or feel the presence of your animal guide. You have a few moments to commune with your guide, who may speak to you or just be with you in silence and in love.

When you feel complete, say goodbye to your animal guide.

Angels

History and mythology are filled with references to angels. They have inspired artists and writers as well as religious leaders. Beyond the myth, angels are real. They carry the essence of innocence and purity and are touched by the hand of God. They are messengers from Spirit. Angels are associated with higher nature, beauty, peace, joy, fulfillment, laughter, and love. They are here to help us heal lost faith and broken trust and innocence, and to lay down the burdens of fear, uncertainty, guilt, pain, and worry. They help to replace feelings of unworthiness and insecurity with those of joy and belonging. Angels assist us in touching a powerful yet gentle force that encourages us to live life to the fullest. They enable us to live with joy instead of fear. Angels help us to enter the world of love. They are different from guides in that they have not lived an earth-time existence: Angels are of the stars, and guides are of the earth. These divine beings have not experienced the earth plane in a human body, so they do not have karma or evolutionary issues to work out. Angels are celestial beings and are of a higher vibrational level than guides. Angels are the essence of purity.

There are many different types of angels, from nature angels to angel messengers to your very own guardian angel, and they can each serve a different function in your life. A nature angel is a guardian or protector of a particular area, such as a mountain; the entire mountain will be under the care and guardianship of one angel. Or a lake can have an angel that watches over it. Different places in nature that have a special feeling are most often under the protective kindness of an angel. There are archangels, such as the Archangel Michael with his sword of truth, that serve as guardians for our entire planet. And there are messenger angels that will sometimes take on human form for brief periods to send a message, to offer help in time of danger, or to teach an important lesson.

People have shared with me remarkable stories about angels both with and without wings; each story carries with it a magical feeling of light and love. One woman, flying home from her vacation, decided to finish her last roll of film by taking pictures of some clouds through the plane window. A few days later she received an urgent phone call from the film processors, who asked her to come down to the shop. When she arrived, they wanted to know how she had produced the images on her cloud pictures. "What images?" she asked. "They are just clouds!" Then they showed her the photos. In the middle of each of her cloud pictures was the most beautiful angel with large golden wings and a radiant smile. She said that the angel looked male, with short brown hair, and was in very clear detail.

One man told me that as a young man he had lived in the country, and on his family's property was a small lake. One day he took a walk by this lake and saw two angels flying back and forth over it. He ran to get his brother, who was eighteen at the time. He said his brother didn't want to come, but he dragged him, and when they got to the lake the angels were still flying back and forth, apparently not noticing him or his brother. They sat and watched the angels for about an hour. Both these stories serve as examples of nature angels.

Another man told me how he broke down on a narrow mountain road during a winter blizzard. A part of his four-wheel-drive truck was broken, and he was miles from any assistance. He had just about given up hope, when a man came along in a truck who just *happened* to have the part that he needed, and helped him pull his truck out of the snow where it had gotten stuck. This man told me that when he turned to thank the man after he got his truck started, not only were the helpful stranger and his vehicle gone, but there were no tire marks in the snow! I have no way of verifying these amazing stories, but the sheer volume of accounts of angels or angelic intervention gives credence to the idea that angels are real and are here to help us.

The guardian angel is a very special being that is with you from the time of your birth. It can help you explore the special gifts that you were born with and find ways of freely expressing those gifts. An angel's main purpose is the transformation of human attitude, always moving it toward the Light.

Angels appear in many different forms. However, the form that most people associate with angels is the traditional church-window angel with wings. Almost every culture in the world has adherents of winged angels. Native Americans called them the Bird People, alluding to their winged appearance. There are accounts of winged angels in ancient Mesopotamia and Assyria. There are angels in Christianity, Buddhism, Taoism, Judaism, Zoroastrianism, and in Islamic tradition. The Vikings called them *valkyries*, the ancient Persians called them *fereshta*, and the Greeks called them *horae*. There are reports of these divine winged creatures all over the world.

More common are reports of angels appearing in human form. These angels appear when they are needed and then disappear. They seem to take a form that is comforting and pleasing to the individual to whom they appear. I have heard numerous reports of the physical appearance of these angelic beings. They appear as both male and female, young and old, of all different races, some well dressed, some shabbily dressed. They all offer guidance and help in a nonintrusive way.

Sometimes an angel will superimpose its energy on a person. When this occurs, the person may unwittingly offer assistance and guidance to someone else in need—*and never even remember it!* It will seem that some tremendous force of goodness takes over momentarily and offers just the right message to another. Of course, there can be many explanations for this, but I believe that it is angelic intervention.

Although some people have reported seeing angels, most angels aren't seen but felt. I have several ways of telling if an angel is present. The wonderful smell of flowers often accompanies their presence. Sometimes they announce their arrival with a slight breeze, even if all the windows are closed. This breeze is the flutter of wings (yes, some angels do have wings!). Sometimes you hear the sound of bells, chimes, or trumpets when they come. I believe that the reason for the apparent sound of trumpets is that when angels break into our dimension, the sound that most closely resembles their entry is that of trumpets. Sometimes a person will think he sees a light, which can indicate the arrival of an angel. But the most usual way is simply the feeling that there is an angel present. You will feel a warm wave of love wash over you. If you think you are in the presence of an angel, you most likely are.

From archangels to your guardian angel, right now all angels are bridging our physical reality with their pure spiritual energy. Like a leaf falling softly on the still pool of our consciousness, with ripples growing outward in ever-larger circles, we will recognize their presence. As we trust, they will pour their blessings on us. They are a doorway to the divine within. Angels have been waiting for us to be ready, and now is the time. The time has arrived for angels to manifest for humanity. I believe that multitudes of angels will make their presence known in the years ahead as we heal old wounds from the past and step into the future. Expect a miracle!

Calling a Guide Before Past-Life Exploration

Before embarking on any past-life exploration, it is valuable to spend a few minutes calling upon your guide or an angel. After you have spent a few minutes relaxing (you can use the guided process that follows), visualize your guide. If you can't get a visual image of your guide, imagine or sense a large, glowing sphere of gold, white, or silver light. Feel yourself surrounded by this bubble of light and love and protection. After you have done this, say to yourself, either out loud or silently: "Dear guardian, I ask for your assistance and guidance as I explore my past lives. Help me understand who I was and why I chose those past lives. Help me to forgive and heal any blockages and barriers that originated in the past. I ask for assistance to heal old emotional wounds and pain, even if I don't consciously remember my journey to the past. I give thanks for your loving blessings." I have found that this invocation produces remarkable results.

Guide Meditation

This meditation can be read or taped to assist you in opening to your guides.

You are about to embark on an exciting journey to that inner place deep within yourself. Once you have tapped in to this inner place, you will have access to an inner source of great strength, power, and peace. You are commencing a journey where you will discover your sanctuary and encounter your master guide. To prepare for this journey across the bridge of time, lie or sit in a comfortable position, with your spine straight and your arms and legs uncrossed.

Do this now . . . Good.

As soon as you are perfectly comfortable, allow your eyes to close softly. Now inhale. Completely fill your lungs with air . . . hold for three seconds . . . and as you exhale, feel yourself relaxing.

Good. Now take another deep breath . . . even deeper than before . . . hold . . . and exhale completely. And, as you exhale, feel your entire body relaxing . . . completely relaxing.

Take one final deep breath and . . . without letting any air out . . . take in even more air and hold. And while you are holding that breath let your body relax. Really feel your body relaxing. Now let the air out. Let it all out . . . completely empty your lungs . . . all the way out . . . all the way out. . . . Relax . . . And as you begin to breathe naturally, notice as your stomach gently rises and falls . . . rises and falls . . . it's as though the entire universe is breathing through you. Just let all your cares and worries float away.

As these gentle, relaxing breaths continue, put your awareness in the middle of your chest. Your vital forces flow freely in and out of the middle of your chest. It's so peaceful to be so gently rocked by this natural rhythm. It feels so good to be aligned with your heart connec-

tion. There is no separation between you and that great force that surges through all of life.

Brilliant currents of vital life-force energy flow in and out through your heart center with each inhalation and exhalation. When you breathe in you are drawing in shimmering, powerful, golden light . . . and when you exhale you radiate that light out to those you love and to the universe.

Your body is very relaxed. The small muscles around your eyes are utterly relaxed and smooth. Your brow is relaxed and tranquil. Your jaw muscles are very relaxed. Your thoughts dissolve and just fade away. An inner glow envelops you. You feel so fluid . . . so whole. Take a deep breath in and out. You feel so loved and lovable.

Again, take one more deep breath in and out . . . let everything go . . . relax. . . . You are in complete harmony with all of life.

Now imagine a very beautiful place in nature. Perhaps it's somewhere that you've been before or somewhere that exists only in your imagination. Spend just a moment imagining this place as real, visualizing as many specific details as possible. For example, if there are flowers in your sanctuary, smell and touch them. Use all your senses to experience this place in nature. Spend some time imagining or sensing that you are walking or running in this place . . . see yourself healthy and carefree. Imagine that you are breathing deeply of the fresh, clean, refreshing air. Somewhere in this place is a clear, still pool. Take a moment to imagine or sense it. It might be a pond with moonlit secrets hidden in its depths, or a spring-fed pool where you can see your own reflection—but altered, as if in a dream. Or perhaps it is a satin, glass-still lake.

As you stand near this still pool, you notice that a mist is forming near it. The spiraling mist begins to form a cloud that hugs the earth. From the center of this cloud you are aware of a faint hum . . . a hum that gets louder and louder . . . a hum that seems to resonate with the very center of your being. Intuitively, you are aware that your master guide is approaching. The very center of this swirling mist is the arrival point for your master guide.

This guide has come forth through the ages to be with you, to guide you and offer you unconditional love and support. Through the mist, you can feel in every cell of your being the all-pervading love and absolute, unconditional acceptance given you by your guide. Your guide is coming forth from the ages to provide you with insight and guidance and love. This being knows you intimately and has been awaiting your call.

Now reach out your hand into the mist. As you do so, be aware of and feel your guide's hand gently slipping into your own. In this moment allow yourself to feel a relaxation so deep that it touches the very core of your being. The mist is beginning to clear and you have the opportunity to meet your master guide. If you are not able to see him or her, get a sense or feeling of your guide.

Greet your guide. Ask your guide's name. Just accept whatever comes forth. Spend some time talking to your guide. Ask if he or she has any special advice for you. Or ask any questions that you might have. Or you may simply want to sit with your guide. You may do this now. Your guide can help you in your past-life explorations or assist you during your dreams. Know that you can visit this place time and time again, and you can visit your guide whenever you want.

Say goodbye to your guide.

At this time you may wish to drift off to sleep. If you want to return to normal waking consciousness, however, simply take a deep breath . . . and in your own time, when you are ready, allow your eyes to open gently.

If you do this guided meditation before sleep, be sure to record your dreams the next morning (see chapter 5). Watch for a loving being appearing in your dreams; even if that being takes different forms, the feeling emanating from it will be the same. Over time these recurring sensations and images will become a familiar indication of your guide's presence. Be alert to these sensations—otherwise, at first you may discount them. The more you open up to, believe in, and interact with your guides, the stronger they become as an integral part of your life.

As you begin to connect with your guides and angels you'll find it much easier to recall past lives. This is because your guides contribute to a feeling of safety while you are exploring past lives in your dreams, in regressions, and in waking life. I find that the best results in past-life regressions occur when an individual feels safe, and this always happens when one is connected with his or her higher guidance. In fact, I find the attendance of a guide so helpful that I rarely do a past-life regression now without calling on their assistance. Their loving presence helps direct the course of the therapy.

8.
PAST LIVES, FUTURE LIVES

One foggy morning, as a small child, I sat forlornly on a rusty swing. My feet barely reached the ground as I shuffled my toes back and forth on the dirt. Suddenly I turned. I thought I had sensed someone approaching, but no one was there. I remember a deep sense of calm and belonging settling over me. I no longer felt alone.

This memory was completely forgotten until some thirty years later, when I was endeavoring to go back in time to visit myself as a small child. I popped out of my imagined time tunnel to find myself comforting a very young Denise as she sat slumped on a rusty swing. I told her I loved her unconditionally. I let her know that she had some tough times ahead, but that she would make it, and her future would be wonderful. As I talked to her, she straightened up and it seemed a heavy weight had been lifted from her spirit.

Coming back into the present time, I was astonished. Not only had I traveled back and visited my younger self, but as a small child I *remembered* the visit! I don't remember someone talking to me that foggy morning, but I remember feeling that someone who cared for me was by my side, and even though I couldn't see whoever it was, I knew that I didn't need to feel lonely anymore. It was a remarkable experience.

Changing the Past

I believe that the future and *the past* are malleable. I have experienced profound changes in my own life and in the lives of others simply by going into the past (either in this life or in past lives) and altering it. You can actually alter the present by altering the past. Remarkably, when you change the present by changing the past, history is created to support the new present. There are many documented cases of individuals in therapy regressing to an earlier time in their lives and healing wounds that occurred at the time. That healing then transforms their present-day lives. Past-life therapy works in an even more extraordinary way. When you go back and release the trauma locked up in previous lifetimes, you can profoundly alter the history of your existence right from the beginning. This may sound unbelievable, but I have seen case after case where individuals in my seminars literally went to the past, changed it, and came back to a changed present. The changes in the past seem to weave themselves through time, creating a new future. I believe that this is a phenomenon whose time has come, and that you will find it appearing more and more often in films and books.

I discussed changing the past and creating a better outcome for yourself in chapter 6. It is the most powerful method for resolution that I know. You no longer need view yourself as a victim—you can take control of your life. You have the power, to make it be the way it should have been!

However, if it seems too philosophical to think about *really* changing the past, just think that you are changing the past that dwells within your mind. All the memories of the past—all the limiting beliefs and negative programming—exist in your mind. Change your mind and change your life. Whether you believe that you are actually changing the past or that you are just changing the past in your mind, it works!

I believe that reality is created by agreement; even the past is created by agreement. If many people agree on something, then it becomes a reality. For example, lots of people agree that Picasso was a great painter. Thus, Picasso was a great painter because people agree on the value of his art. If no one had ever agreed on this, then Picasso would not be a great painter.

I believe that form, too, coalesces around our collective beliefs and agreements. For example, the world used to be flat. At a certain time in our history, everyone agreed that the world was flat. All the evidence available at the time proved that the world was always flat. Now the world is round. All our scientific evidence proves that this is so—and it proves that the world was *always* round. If, in the future, it was proved that the earth is actually a hologram projected from another universe, all the scientific evidence would prove that the world was a hologram—and that it had always been a hologram.

I believe that we are constantly changing not just our present, but our past and our future as well, from any given point in time. I believe that the universe is a pulsating, fluctuating ocean of consciousness with all time occurring simultaneously. We are all intimately connected in this sea of consciousness. When you release an old blockage through changing your perception of the past, not only does it help you, but it is like a pebble dropped in a still pool whose ripples are felt at the farthest shore. Not only are your immediate family and friends affected positively by the "ripples," but so is everyone else on the planet who shares your frequencies—even if they don't know you.

The Ripple Effect

Here is an example of how this ripple effect works. Daniel came to me because he was having problems with money. He would put time and effort into a project, but his financial gain would be disproportionately small. Daniel was very discouraged and felt that there must be some inner blockage causing the problem. He regressed to a life in the Middle East in which he was a merchant (he is of Middle Eastern descent in this life). In his past life he wasn't always fair in his business practices. In Daniel's regression he recalled a very traumatic event that was motivated by his past-life business interactions.

It was a searing day, the heat permeating every corner and every fold of life. Though the darkness of the merchant's home offered some respite from the heat, the lengthening shadows of the approaching evening were welcome. The merchant looked lovingly at his young son, who had just come in from outside.

Suddenly the merchant felt a presence in the doorway. He looked up. Menacingly filling the doorway, a man towered over him. It was a man whom the merchant knew only slightly. In an instant, however, the merchant understood why the man was there. Recently the merchant had unfairly gotten the better of him in a business transaction.

Seeming in slow motion, the man in the doorway raised a dagger high above his head and rushed forward. In one silken movement he slit the throat of the merchant's son . . . and then ran out.

The scene was so traumatic that Daniel immediately came out of his regression. I said, "As painful as it seems, you can go back into that scene and change it. Doing this will have a positive and powerful effect on your present life."

Reluctantly he went back into the past life. He replayed the scene until the man in the doorway held the knife high overhead. He then changed the scene and imagined the man dropping the knife and running away. I said, "Go forward in your life as a merchant." He then saw himself treating people very fairly. His reputation as a man of honor spread throughout the land. He saw himself growing old and becoming more prosperous with each passing year. He saw his son growing up to become a fine young man and an honorable merchant like his father.

As a result of exploring and changing his past-life memories, two things occurred. Daniel's business immediately began to turn around and he is now very prosperous. The second event was extraordinary: In Daniel's regression he saw that his teenage son in his present life was also the son who was killed in his Middle Eastern life. His present-life son had had a constant sore throat from the time that he was a small boy (most likely, unresolved trauma from having died from a slit throat). The moment when Daniel changed his past life, his son's sore throat went away, and it has not returned although some eight years have passed. This is particularly interesting in light of the fact that Daniel had never told his family about the regression, because he thought they wouldn't understand about that kind of therapy.

When Daniel changed the past and released an old blockage, it had a ripple effect on those around him—even though they didn't know what he had done. This ripple effect influences not only those around you but everyone else on the same frequency. It could be that, after Daniel's regression, halfway around the world there was another individual who shared his same frequency, who was also struggling with money problems. The next morning she could have awakened feeling that a heavy burden had been lifted, although she didn't know why. We are connected. When one is uplifted, we are all uplifted.

I'm often asked if, when we change the past, we can make a mistake that could influence others in a negative way. I have never seen this occur. I believe that there is a divine guiding force in life that makes sure that when you change the past during regression, it contributes only good to everyone.

Future Lives

Some people find it valuable to visit their future lives or to have their future selves come back through time and space to give advice and guidance based on what they gained in the future. I often do a future-life process in my seminars, and many people are excited about what they discover. Because the time/space veil is thinning, it is becoming easier to travel in your meditations not only to the past but to the future. Some people find that their inner confidence is renewed after they have viewed future triumphs. Others find that they can avoid a difficult future by observing future possibilities and making present-day corrections.

Sometimes, people are concerned about how they will cope if they see something truly terrible in their future, or in the future of someone they love. The future is as malleable as the past, and what you will see is a future probability. Fortunately, you are in a position to alter that probability.

The process used to travel to future lives is similar to that used to access past lives. The following meditation will help you get started.

First, allow yourself to become very relaxed. You might deepen your breath or imagine a favorite place in nature. Imagine yourself sitting against a willow tree as you listen to a bubbling stream nearby. Allow your entire body to become very relaxed, placing awareness on every part of your body. Let every part of your body relax as you fill each and every part with tranquillity. Know that every breath is allowing you to become more relaxed. Imagine that your guide is nearby. You have nothing to fear. You are at peace with the universe. You are surrounded by infinite love.

See yourself surrounded in a protective bubble of white light. You are very safe and protected. As you are sitting in nature, day turns to night. One by one the stars come out. The entire sky becomes filled with shimmering, luminous stars. One particular star takes your attention. As you watch, the star becomes brighter and brighter. It slowly begins to float down from the sky. It is moving toward you.

As it gets closer you can see that it is actually a spherical vehicle made of light and sound. It looks like a large, luminous bubble. You know this is a time machine.

As you step inside, you feel comforted by the lush, cocoonlike interior. Quietly, with only the softest hum, the vehicle lifts from the earth and begins to float gently. As you settle back into the soft cushions, you observe the entire canopy of stars through the windows.

You feel your vehicle floating gently back to earth. As you step out of your time machine, you find yourself by a beautiful, still pool. As you gaze into it you begin to have visions. You see a vision of who you are in a future life. Notice whether you are male or female. Notice any people who look similar to your present-day friends or family. Scan your future life and note the area of greatest conflict. You are free to change the scene you are observing. In addition, see if there is anything in your present life that you can do to avert this future possibility. Surround the entire scene with infinite love and return to your time machine. Begin to bring yourself to normal waking consciousness. You know that all that you have seen of your future was for your highest good, and you know that you are making the necessary adjustments in your present life to create an exciting, fulfilling future.

9.

TIME, SPACE, AND BEYOND: THE NEXT STEP

I believe that our past, present, and future lives are not sequential but are all occurring at the same time. However, because we are linear beings and because we experience our lives in terms of past, present, and future, I have discussed our lives in this book as if they occur in a sequential manner.

To help you understand this idea of concurrent lives, imagine a faceted mirrored ball hanging above a circular ballroom and radiating reflections throughout it. As the ball moves, the individual reflections move around the room. Pick one reflection and place your awareness on it. Imagine that the reflection on which you have focused is you and your current life.

You appear to be going forward. The scenes around you are changing as you seem to be going forward in time. There are other reflections in front of you as well as behind you. The reflections that are behind you as you move around the room are your past lives. They seem to be past lives because they are seemingly behind you. The reflections seemingly in front of you are your future lives. They are seemingly moving through time as well.

The distances between the reflections in front of you and the reflections behind you seem to stay constant—perhaps two feet between you and the closest reflection behind you, and three feet between you and the reflection in front. Given that you are in a perfectly round room, those distances will remain constant even though the mirrored ball is moving. This gives credence to the illusion that time is fixed because, no matter where your reflection has traveled in the ballroom, there is always two feet between you and the nearest reflection behind you and three feet in front. This is measurable and constant.

Looking at this in terms of past lives and future lives, if one foot is equal to a hundred years, then it might seem that there are two hundred years between your current life and your most recent past life and three hundred years between your present life and your next future life. However, as you move up the beam of light toward the mirrored ball (which is the source of your reflection), the closest reflections in front of and behind you change, and the distances become much shorter. This demonstrates how the separations between past, present, and future are diminishing. The more we collectively move toward our Source, the more our perceptions of time and space will begin to change. The closer you move to the Source, the more diminished the boundaries between past, present, and future will seem.

Here is another way to perceive the thinning of the boundaries of time: Imagine that if you left your individual mirrored-ball reflection and traveled forward in time, eventually you would come full circle and reach your past lives. Likewise, if you traveled backward in time, eventually you would come full circle and reach your future lives.

All the reflections on the ballroom wall seem separate and individual. Some reflections seem like future lives, some like past lives, and some can be thought of as other people's lives. However, if you traveled from your individual reflection to the Source, the mirrored ball, you would see that all lives—past, present, and future—all people, and all matter are resonating from the same Source. We are not separate from anyone else. Neither are we separate from what we call the "past" and the "future." All lives are coexisting, intertwined and dependent on each other right now.

Time is not an absolute. It is Infinite Eternity, arbitrarily divided into portions called centuries, years, months, weeks, days, hours, seconds, and so on. In the past we thought of time as steady and nonchanging. I believe that the more you explore the universes within yourself, through meditation or other spiritual practices, the more fluid time becomes. You can actually perceive time speeding up or slowing down. Time is a product of your perception. The only "time" that actually exists is the time that you are perceiving. When you are involved in something creative, "time flies by," and an hour seems but a blink of an eye. By contrast, when you are waiting for a friend who is an hour late, time can seem to stretch for an eternity.

You can speed up time or slow down time subjectively. This is what I call entering "hypertime," an expression I coined because it most accurately describes this phenomenon. *Webster's New Collegiate Dictionary* defines *hyper* as "that which exists in a space of more than three dimensions." Entering hypertime is literally stepping into "time that dwells beyond the three dimensions." In my Journeys into Past Lives seminars, I teach participants how to enter hypertime. I use powerful breathing and movement techniques that I have developed to "snap-shift" perceptual reality in order to enter into hypertime.

I have heard remarkable stories from seminar participants who have integrated these time techniques into their lives. One woman shared the following story with me: For eighteen years she had worked at the same job. To get there she always drove the same route at the same speed, and usually there was never much variation in traffic conditions. It almost always took her exactly forty-seven minutes to get from home to work. She told me that after participating in my seminar, she decided to use the techniques that I had taught. She entered hypertime before she left for work, but otherwise she did everything exactly the same as always. Yet, she got to work in thirty-two minutes! This is not an unusual story. Many participants of my seminars have reported similar events in their lives.

Given the current laws that govern our physical world, it should be impossible to alter time in such a manner. But what if time really is fluid? Suppose time contracts and expands in a rhythmically pulsating universe? Suppose time is a function of our perception? Imagine that we can dramatically shift our perception and enter into the timeless Source, from which all beingness emanates. Suppose we could travel to the dimensionless regions where time and space are born? Given these suppositions, we could in fact alter time. I believe that these suppositions *are* true. I believe each and every one of us is both the perceiver and the definer of "time."

My near-death experience led me on a quest for self-understanding and to find my way back "home" again. After I returned to my body, I intuitively knew there was a way to get back to the Light without dying; there was a way to "be home" and still exist in a physical body. I knew there were countless dimensions coexisting with the physical dimension, and we could be aware of them by tuning an inner "dial." Just as right now there are numerous radio stations flooding your home or office, but you can't hear them unless you have your radio tuned in, we need only to find our inner dial and tune in.

Most people think of the place that you go to when you die as "heaven." We subconsciously think of heaven as somewhere way up above the clouds. But heaven/home isn't up in the sky. It's here—now. It is a dimension coexisting with our physical reality. One way you can know that you are close to that dimension is through synchronicity—for example, when you think of something and it happens; you need something and it appears; you think of someone and he or she calls. When I was in the Light, there was no time between thought and creation. My thoughts were instantly manifest. The closer you get to that dimension, the faster your thoughts become manifest in the physical world.

There is nothing out there that isn't you. Because of the linear way that we perceive reality, I don't think we can ever understand this intellectually, communicate about it verbally, or even write about it in a comprehensive way. However, I believe that deep inside, *we all do know this*. Deep inside, we have all experienced this feeling. Even in the most fulfilled human being there is a longing, a yearning, and a remembering of that exquisite place of oneness and unity.

Each and every part of the universe is a part of you. You are the most astonishing blend imaginable. We usually identify with our bodies and feel separate from all the other parts of ourselves. Sometimes we identify with our children or even our possessions (a man will run into a burning building to rescue valuables because in that moment he is identifying himself more with the valuables than with his body). But in fact you are living in a miraculous ocean of energy, and each part of that flow of energy is you. You might imagine all these parts as making up a gigantic orchestra of energy. When there is a harmonization of all these parts, a vibration is created that resonates throughout the universe.

This is what my Native American ancestors meant when they talked about being in "right relation" with all things. It means to honor and respect the livingness in all things. It means to honor the animal or plant that gives you life. It means to honor all life around you. It means to listen, *really listen*, and honor the reality of your neighbors, for they are not separate from you. They *are* you!

To be in right relation with all things means living in harmony with all other parts of the collective Spirit. One way to do this is to move toward accepting, unconditionally, the reality of others. This also means moving toward acceptance of all parts of yourself, especially the parts that you have judged negatively, and even what you were in your past lives. Being in right relation means helping others wherever you can, without expecting anything in return. It means acting with compassion toward all other parts of the life force. Know that there is no less life in your typewriter than in the beautiful apple tree that grows outside your window. Honor, accept, and love the life that is all around you, for it is all you in different forms. Whatever you judge sets you further along the path of separateness. Whatever you love allows the orchestra of all your parts (which in its totality is God) to vibrate and sing with joy throughout the universe.

May Great Spirit that is both within you and all around you bless you in all that you do, so that all of your dreams in all of your lifetimes may manifest joy for all of us here, together forever in the magnificent, ever-expanding universe.

Further Information

Denise offers professional certification training programs in Interior Alignment© as well as seminars and workshops on other subjects.

For information about Denise's audio tapes and seminars, contact:
Denise Linn Seminars
P.O. Box 75657
Seattle, Washington 98125-0657

For a Sacred Space Products Catalog, contact:
P.O. Box 75036
Seattle, Washington 98125-0036

About the Author

DENISE LINN'S personal journey began as a result of a near-death experience at age seventeen. Her life-changing experiences and remarkable recovery set her on a spiritual quest that led her to study the healing traditions of many cultures, including those of her own Cherokee ancestors. Her quest took her to a Hawaiian kahuna (shaman), Reiki Master Hawayo Takata, the Aborigines in the Australian bush, and the Zulus in Bophuthatswana. She was also adopted into a New Zealand Maori tribe. In addition, Denise lived in a Zen Buddhist monastery for over two years.

Denise is an international lecturer, healer, and originator of Interior Alignment, and she holds regular seminars on six continents. She is the author of *Sacred Space* and *The Secret Language of Signs*, and appears extensively on television and radio programs throughout the world.